About the Author

David Harper is a BBC TV antiques presenter, artist, speaker, historian, and writer.

A Bash with The British Empire

David Harper

A Bash with The British Empire

Olympia Publishers
London

www.olympiapublishers.com
OLYMPIA PAPERBACK EDITION

A CIP catalogue record for this title is
available from the British Library.

ISBN: 978-1-80074-858-3

First Published in 2023

Olympia Publishers
Tallis House
2 Tallis Street
London
EC4Y 0AB
Printed in Great Britain

Dedication

Dedicated to my adventurous parents

.

Acknowledgements

With thanks to the illustrator, William Crawford Designs.
Motor Car illustrations by David Harper.

Introduction

'A Bash with The British Empire' takes a funny and a fresh look at the real people of the empire. The celebrities, the everyday general public, their odd habits, customs and even their fashion mistakes! Also, the rulers, the decision makers, the money makers, and the rule breakers! We'll visit the exotic places, marvel at the mad inventions, the eccentricities, the mistakes, and disasters, but also the successes and benefits, all of which built and shaped not only the greatest empire the world has ever seen, but one, which you'll discover, has shaped your life too…! Yes, the British Empire has influenced all of our lives much more than we ever knew!

Empires are nothing new of course, they've been around forever. From the Mongol empire in Asia with their founder Genghis Khan, who wasn't averse to killing several million people, to the Mughals who dominated India for a few hundred years to the Portuguese and Spanish who colonised South America and of course, the most famous of them all, the Romans in Europe and the Middle East. They were all, in countless ways thought of today as dastardly, but of course, they were of their time.

All empires are products of their time and should really be viewed as such and not through the current lens of sensibility. They lived by the modern rules of their day, as we do today and I often wonder how easy it would be, in a few hundred years' time, for people, our descendants, to look back upon us with utter distain at the way we lived our lives? For example, we still have slavery in the world, currently around 40 million enslaved people, and countries that turn a blind eye to it today, will be judged by history later, as may anyone complicit in fuelling the illegal drug trade. Users, suppliers, governments that rely on tax revenue from companies, known to be laundering cash from the trade, could easily be judged harshly! And the list could go on… we're not perfect today you know, no matter how hard some people try to tell us they themselves are!

The very idea of any sort of all powerful and controlling empire, is of course hated now, but travel back in time and you'll discover that the past, as they say, is a very different country!

If the British hadn't had the confidence (some say arrogance… there's a fine line between the two!) to create their massive empire, they would have been subjugated by any number of other nations around the world and much more malignant ones too. From far away and close to home.

It was a race to the top to build the biggest and most powerful empire before anyone else… and at the time, the British won that race.

For Britain, the timing of the building of her empire was just right. Britons certainly had the confidence required, the ability, the know-how and crucially, the financial wherewithal to do it. This was funded by the industrial revolution. That revolution, which they themselves instigated, cultivated and invented made Britain into the workshop of the world and that brought in the cash flow required to also make Britain ruler of the seas, the most powerful nation in the world and subsequently the self-appointed policeman of the world!

The money, the power, the prestige and the seemingly never-ending audacity and success of the British made them international friends and admirers, as well as enemies in equal measures… both then and now, at home and abroad.

You could, if you like, use the classic Marmite (British invention) analogy here. Love it or hate it!

And on the empire 'top trumps' measuring system, the British Empire wasn't just the most powerful the world had ever known, but it holds the record for being the largest empire the world has ever seen too. Almost twenty-five percent of the earth's surface and its population were once ruled over by the British Empire. To get that into some sort of perspective, Britain's total land mass is around eighty thousand square miles. This includes England, Wales, Scotland and Northern Ireland. At the height of the empire, Britain controlled thirteen million square miles of land. That's over one hundred and sixty times the size of Britain… no wonder that no matter how hard it tried, the sun was never able to set on the British Empire!

Roughly speaking the British Empire lasted around three hundred and fifty years. As with all empires, they take a long time to develop, to expand and spread, and almost as long to come to an end. Several generations either side of their peak… the peak for the British being the tail end of Queen Victoria's reign (1837–1901) so the late 19th century and into the early part of the 20th century.

Things started to go wrong though in 1914 due to the outbreak of World War I. The Great War, that war to end all wars, over the four years it lasted, put a huge strain financially and otherwise on the empire. Loans to fund the war, saw Britain's debt, by the end of it in 1918 increase by a massive ten-fold. This was bad enough, but twenty-one short years later, another financial shock came to rock Britain and her empire in the form of World War II.

Fighting solidly for six years from 1939 to 1945 in the biggest and most crucial war in history, right across her empire and in all corners of the world, pretty well bankrupted and shattered Britain. Britain's imperial power began to collapse due to this perfect storm of war debt, responsibilities to other nations and infrastructure rebuilding costs at home.

On the upside though, the British and her empire were instrumental in defeating the Nazi's and winning the war. But the cost of this was the loss of the empire. It was though, a price worth paying, when you consider this. Had it not been for the British and those from across the empire, Nazi Germany would have likely won the war. Had this been the case, the world today and our recent history would be a very different and unimaginable place indeed.

After the war, the colonies were one by one beginning to demand their independence. Britain didn't fight any colonial wars to keep hold of her dominions, so the hand overs and period of decolonisation was pretty peaceful, and the empire slowly but surely turned into the Commonwealth of Nations. The Commonwealth still makes up a quarter of the world's land mass, but some of the original member states have left the club — The Gambia and Zimbabwe as examples. Others, though, who were never part of the empire, later requested to join and were accepted. Rwanda, who was colonised by Belgium and Germany, but never Britain joined in 2009 and Mozambique, with its Portuguese connections joined in 2005. Out of interest, half of the top twenty global emerging cities, are located within Commonwealth countries. They're all in either India, Africa, or the Far East.

The final major transfer of sovereignty was the hand-over of Hong Kong to the Chinese on 1st July 1997… this, some say is the official date the British Empire came to an end… but, before the last Union Jack was lowered on the stroke of midnight on that summer's evening six thousand miles away from Britain, before Prince Charles gave a farewell speech on behalf of Queen Elizabeth II, the last of the British Empire monarchs and before the party kicked off that night at the Hong Kong Convention and Exhibition Centre in 1997, the British and their empire spent a few hundred years moulding and changing the world forever. Not only linguistically, but with her systems of government and law as well as culturally. Many say of course, this was for the worse and others say for the better… the truth is, both sides of the argument are right. Whatever your opinion, remember that The British Empire, like every empire before it, was of its time… times were different then. It's popular today to shout at history — history, no matter how much people want to change it and demand answers from it, it won't answer back, and although history can be re-interpreted, some things can't be changed.

History is marvellous though if you treat it with reverence. It can be funny, utterly shocking and entertaining 'there's nowt funnier than folk' (as they say in Yorkshire) History is all about real people and their actions in their own unique time… all now long gone. But as well as history being a fascinating read, it's also the best teacher we have. Look back in time and you'll find that not much is new in modern life. Something similar has invariably happened before and history, although it can't shout back at you, it will happily whisper some very good advice!

This book generally takes a lighter look at the period and is full of adventures, calamities, successes, and life changing discoveries from the time of The British Empire. Get to know it's people and how they lived their lives.

Here's some stories, surprising events, and shocking facts you probably didn't know?

Let's start with fashion

Corsets and the Empire Silhouette!

The fashionable look and figure shape for ladies during the mid to late 19th century was that of the classic hourglass. For modesty reasons, almost all of the female form was covered up with clothing, but the figure, or the silhouette, as it was referred to, was of course very visible and the fashion of the time was designed to show that off. And like today, there were lots of tricks that could be employed to enhance certain areas and disguise others! Shoulders and hips were extended artificially with pads under the garments. This gave the impression of a much narrower and pinched waist, which is vital to create the hourglass shape.

That was all well and good, but if the waistline was able to be squeezed as tightly as possible too, then the empire silhouette would be even more dramatic and impressive. Something then, was needed to pull the waistline in and that something of course was the corset… but this was not like any corset you've ever experienced… or at least, I hope not! Corset wearers of the British Empire took its principal design to its limits. Men, by the way were not averse to wearing a corset, but it was the ladies of the time that were known for pulling their corsets so tight, they occasionally died in pursuit of the perfect empire silhouette!

To create that ideal figure for the period, the corset was 'tight laced'. The term describes the practise perfectly well. It was a simple case of pulling the laces of the corset quite tight to suck in the waist, or that's what you might imagine. Tightlacing was actually taking the act of hauling in a corset to its very limits… and its limits, it was discovered were quite remarkable!

Tight laced corset… I'll get onto the topic of Empire tattoos soon!

Dieting was an option to pinch the waist in and get the midriff measurements down and this was popular with some, but the results were not nearly enough for others, so unnaturally squeezing the waist, compressing it down to the smallest measurement possible could only be done by forceful tightlacing. Many ladies became consumed with the idea of the tiniest waist imaginable, and some were even addicted to the painful act of extreme tightlacing and so embarked upon what they called 'corset training' over long periods of time.

So, it wasn't as simple as just squashing the body into a tiny corset. It didn't work that way. To get the perfect silhouette and minuscule waist, the actual body shape itself would need to be changed and re-moulded. This took a lot of time, effort, and practise. First of all, a lady (known as a 'tight lacer') would start the process by wearing a corset with a four-inch smaller waist measurement than that of her natural size. She'd breath in deeply and strap herself in tightly. The feel of the constricting corset took time getting used to, and she'd have to wear this size day and night in an attempt to customise herself to the waist crushing garment — and when I say customise, I mean that literally. The body's internal organs were being squashed at the same time as the waistline and diagrams from the period, show how these organs were actually getting rearranged by the act of squeezing in the midriff. They were getting pushed up and down, below and above the new developing waist!

Once the wearer had grown accustomed to the first tight corset and the body had begun to change its shape, which may take several months of painful tightlacing, an even smaller corset could be introduced, and the process started again. By all accounts, reducing the waist measurement by up to six inches, if you had the commitment, was relatively speaking, easy. To reduce the measurement any more was an awful lot harder. It would now take around a year of continual extreme tightlacing and a lot of discomfort to reduce the waist by a further inch. For some, this became their life's work and for others, it cost them their lives!

…and if not death, at least bad bouts of indigestion!

Anyway, there are many accounts of ladies who took this cosmetic body modification to beyond its reasonable limits. Even though articles were regularly published in medical journals and the newspapers about the dangers of tightlacing, some fashionista ladies were so obsessed with reducing their waist measurement, that they took no notice whatsoever of the warnings. The tight lacer expected constant discomfort, shortness of breath (many feinted at balls and social get togethers due to their corsets being too tight). Indigestion, digestion problems and general stomach complaints were normal, as was excruciating back pain and organ damage.

But still they couldn't stop… that is, until their corset killed them!

It was known that several women had literally crushed themselves to death over a period of time and with one young lady, who died unexpectedly, it was discovered during the autopsy, that two of the metal stays that made up part of the construction of the corset had been rubbing together, quite obviously for some time. This had sharpened the ends of both metal pieces to resemble miniature and razor-sharp spears… An unlucky wrong movement, had the doctors concluded sent one of the corsets metal rods straight through the unfortunate young woman's heart!

There was also the unfortunate case of a showman at the time, a famous female impersonator — drag queen — and hugely popular with his fans, who fainted one night after his stage performance and later died. The term 'Drag Queen' is nothing new. You can thank the 19th century British theatre going public for coming up with that particular nick name. The Empire loved a good drag act and it's believed the origin of the word came about due to the male act wearing and dragging behind him across the stage floor, much to the amusement of the audience, an oversized lady's dress!

Joseph Hennella was around forty years old and had been performing his act as a woman for many years. Throughout those years, he'd worn a corset and tight laced it especially for the show. However, it was said that in the years running up to his death, Joseph had put quite a lot of weight on, due to too many after-show, late night dinners! Therefore, the tightlacing needed to be more and more dramatic to pull in his expanding midriff and maintain the feminine silhouette for his theatre show. Too much tightening though was what caused the collapse in his dressing room that night and later, due to kidney complications brought on by many years of tightlacing, his untimely death… doctors agreed that the over tightened corset he was wearing that night brought on his collapse and his kidney failure was without doubt caused by years of ever tightening tightlacing.

And it wasn't just the medical profession who abhorred tightlacing either. The church too was mightily against the practise. To some people, the use of corsets in this way had become an abomination against God and all that was righteous. Many anti-corset women were vocally outspoken about the harm the fashion of tightlacing was doing to the morals of other women of all classes and all ages (as it wasn't just the very young that were at it)!

Soon, an almost militant, anti-corset movement began called the 'Victorian Dress Reform' and it called for females to adopt a more (in their eyes) sensible and lady like approach to fashion. They demanded something a little more pious ideally and begged women to wear more comfortable, healthier, and less provocative clothing… bearing in mind, this was a period in our history when if a lady showed a bare ankle in public, it was seen as shocking, so I'm not sure whether provocative was the right description!

The movement, very helpfully produced samples of clothing it recommended ladies should wear (none of which were very appealing) and the organisation displayed these in shop windows as examples of how the ideal Victorian lady of the empire should really dress. As well as this, the reform group, helpfully printed out sewing patterns for home clothing manufacture, in the hope that those ladies it tempted to think about reforming, would then discard their fashionable outfits (in fact throw them away) and burn their damnable corsets! Once they'd done this, it was hoped, the cured women might sit at home, follow the sewing patterns provided and make themselves their own 'sensible' and reform vetted clothing! These practical designs provided by the 'Victorian Dress Reform' were referred to by them as 'rational dress' for ladies, which pretty much meant, highly boring, dull, unflattering, and unattractive outfits. Definitely no corsets allowed, and a natural, unmodified waistline was absolutely insisted upon. These demands, generally, filled most fashionable ladies with abject horror! The colours and cuts of the designs recommended to wear for any upstanding lady of honour and good virtue, were described as being ageing and uncomplimentary to say the very least… which was just perfect, according to the reformers!

Apart from occasionally crushing their wearers to death, corsets also gained a reputation for dreadful fashion malfunctions. One of which only occurred when visiting foreign parts. Bearing in mind, this was the height of the British Empire. Many thousands of Britons travelled out into its distant lands and along with the obvious dangers of such long-distance travel, over land and sea, other calamities in the form of fashion faux pas also caused problems. Corsets, worn when travelling abroad proved tricky for some ladies of fashion and so they learnt to adapt them for varying climatic conditions. Steel stays had long since replaced the traditional whale bone in the corsets, which gave them their shape and rigidity. Steel was fine if you lived in Britain, with its temperate climate. However, travelling through the tropics or worse, the jungle, wearing a British made corset, with steel supports could cause fashion and social disasters of the most horrific kind. The kind of thing, only nightmares are made of! You see, the terrible humidity in some parts of the far-flung empire made the steel in the corset sweat and eventually rust. Mixed also with the humidity was the perspiration pouring out of the delicate ladies themselves. Most ladies denied ever sweating, but in these conditions, it was difficult to pretend not to! The combination of the two was terrible. Dripping rust-coloured damp patches would eventually appear. This not only ruined an expensive corset, but the brown stains which wept through the outer garments, caused the most dreadful discolouration patches you can imagine… this was not a good look!

The mass use of corsets during the empire period spawned two terms we often use today. 'Strait-laced' is the first one. This implied a lady was upstanding and proper. Remember, that for a lady to remove her corset, a lot of time and effort was required, so a strait-laced lady was unlikely (and unable) to be whipping her clothes off at the 'drop of a hat' (a great saying that originates from the days of empire and appears later on in this book under 'empire sayings'). Her appearance and gait were also, due to the tightly strung corset, rigid, which gave an impression of high morals. So, a strait-laced lady was prim, proper, formal and incorruptible.

On the other hand, a 'loose woman' implies exactly the opposite of the above! This described a lady who wore no corset and had a reputation for being slovenly and free and easy with the removing of her clothing and her affections!

The moral evil of corsets (as some saw them) began to fall out of fashion towards the end of the 19th century. It was no doubt just a natural progression in fashion, but the pressures from the reformers probably speeded it up. The reformers were joined in their criticism by more and more doctors, preachers and journalists, all of whom condemned as they said at the time 'the vanity and frivolity of women, who would sacrifice the health and compromised fertility, for the sake of fashion'.

In the early 20th century, the contemporary bra as we know it today began to emerge and much looser clothing, with more of a natural waistline started to become fashionable (which no doubt saved some lives). The corset survived of course, but it now, strangely, gained a reputation amongst the 'strait-laced' in society as being a garment that had entered the world of fetish… which made it even more appealing to some!

Now is the perfect time to introduce the amazing Ethel Granger. Born in England in 1905, Ethel was a famous corset 'tight lacer' who, over many years, wearing ever smaller corsets, day and night, along with specially made heavy metal bands, reduced her waist through body modification down to a world record circumference of thirteen inches. She was quite a shocker in her day and in 1955, she made it into the very first publication of The Guinness Book of Records, who confirmed her overall figure measurements to be an astonishing hourglass shaped 36-13-38!

As well as body modification, Ethel was famous for her body piercings (in most places!) and even went out to do her daily shopping wearing a septum ring… this was seriously shocking stuff during the latter days of the British Empire!

Tattoos

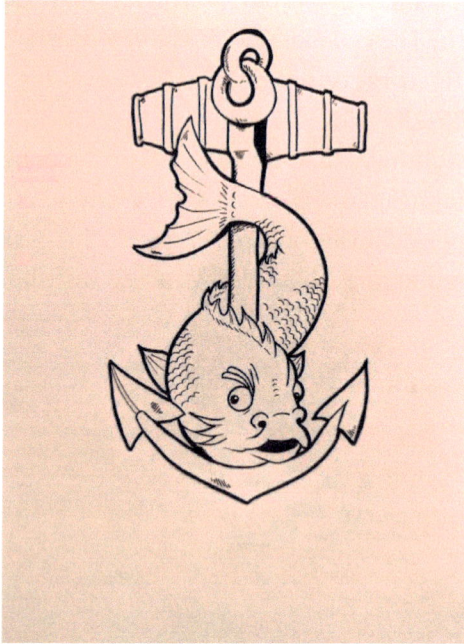

Fish and anchor tattoo. A popular 19th century design

You know that tattoos are nothing new and that they're incredibly popular now in the 21st century, but their history during the days of the empire is a fascinating and little known one.

Cultures around the world have been tattooing themselves for as long as history itself, with evidence that can be traced back tens of thousands of years. And, in recent times (historically speaking) the ancestors of the British empire builders, the Anglo Saxons were very keen on tattoos too. Records from visitors to Britain often comment on the locals colourfully decorated tattoos and unusual patterns woven around their bodies — It is said that King Harold II, the last Anglo-Saxon king, who was killed at the Battle of Hastings in 1066 had the name of his wife, 'Edith' tattooed across his chest. Some records even say that the tattoo was the only way anyone could officially identify his badly trampled and hacked body after the battle. And in the 17th century, British pilgrims visiting the Holy Lands often had the cross tattooed on their body to commemorate their visit. And we all know that sailors are famous for tattooing images of ports they'd visited throughout their sea faring careers. Anchors, countries, ships, mermaids and girls' names were common too for the seafarers, but did you know that many sailors tattooed their feet for good luck? One foot with an image of a pig and the other with a rooster. It's known that neither a pig, nor a rooster like to swim, and both are known to panic in water and make great attempts to get out of the stuff if they fall into it. Barely any sailors were ever able to swim either and so the fear of falling into the sea was naturally great. Sailors are a superstitious bunch and superstition had it that the pig and the rooster would help get the sailor to dry land, pretty sharpish, if he fell overboard!

Another little known fact is this — It was the famous empire explorer and sailor, Captain James Cook, who made three voyages to the South Pacific in the 1760s and '70s who is credited with introducing the word 'tattoo' into the English language. On their return to Britain, Captain Cook and his men (Cook didn't return after his third visit, as he was killed in

Hawaii by natives) the sailors told adventurous tales of their encounters with the peoples from these exotic islands in Polynesia, who were painted head to foot in something described by the locals there as 'tattow'… the term stuck and it's easy to see how this word quickly became 'tattoo'.

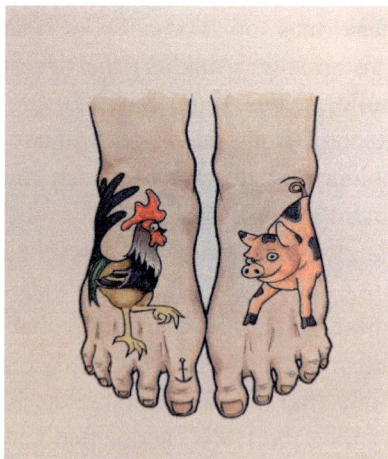

Here's a quote from Captain Cook at the time, writing in his journal after witnessing natives getting tattooed:

"Both sexes paint their Bodys, Tattow, as it is called in their Language. This method of Tattowing I shall now describe… As this is a painful operation, especially the Tattowing of their Buttocks, it is performed but once in their Lifetimes." Cook continues to talk about the method employed by the natives to carry out their tattooing and mentions the patterns and colours used to mark the body. Not much has changed today and by all accounts, it's still as painful!

Prior to the introduction of the word tattoo which we all understand, the act of permanently decorating one's body was referred to as being 'pricked', 'marked', 'engraved', 'decorated', 'punctured', 'stained', or even 'embroidered'.

Plenty of Captain Cook's sailors themselves were tattooed whilst out in Polynesia, including and quite surprisingly his science officer and expedition botanist, Sir Joseph Banks, who was a highly regarded member of the English aristocracy. It's interesting to note that Sir Joseph was also around a hundred years ahead of his time, when it came to fashion and tattoos!

The act of tattooing became highly popular throughout British society, but it was mainly associated with the rougher end of it. The lower classes, the sailors and of course, the criminals. So, tattoos didn't have a great reputation amongst the higher echelons. That is until the 1870s when it became fashionable amongst the upper classes (a hundred years after Sir Joseph's first tattoo) and right across Europe too. The fad spread like wildfire, especially right at the top of society, amongst the British aristocracy. The aristocrats really fell in love with tattoos, and it was estimated in 1898 that around one in five of the gentry had at least one tattoo!

Once dressed in Victorian modesty clothing, you'd never know the tattoos existed!

Royalty fell under the spell of the tattoo as well. King Edward VII (the son of the apparently very strait-laced Queen Victoria) had tattoos, as did his son and later King George V, as well as George's cousin (who bizarrely looked like his twin) Tsar Nicholas II of Russia... they all had them, including some cracking and elaborate interpretations of their own particular Royal family crests!

The first officially recognised tattoo studio with a professional resident tattooist to exist in Britain was on Jermyn Street, London.

It was opened in the 1880s by a chap named Sutherland Macdonald. The location of the studio, right in the centre of London, was ideal and appropriate. The cost of having a professional tattoo was not only paid for in discomfort, but very expensive too financially. Sutherland knew his market. He catered for wealthy, upper-class clients who had the money and loved getting tattooed... and that part of London is where they congregated.

He also trained a chap called George Burchett, who became known throughout the empire as 'The King of Tattooists' and eventually, the most famous tattoo artist in the world. George was a true maverick. He was expelled from school at the age of twelve for tattooing classmates in lessons! With few choices in life, he joined the Royal Navy at thirteen, travelled the world and practised his hobby on willing fellow seaman aboard ship. A few years later, he absconded from the navy and found himself in London, penniless and looking for work. He found Sutherland and his tattoo studio, Sutherland employed him, and George got the opportunity to put his hobby and talents to good use. After some guidance, training, and fine tuning of his tattooing skills in Sutherland's tattoo parlour, George eventually set up his own studio, also in London and the boy who was kicked out of school at twelve, soon became the celebrity go-to tattoo artist for the rich and famous of the day, including European Royalty, like the King of Denmark, the King of Sweden and apparently, our very own King George V!

The missing tattoo: There was a fascinating criminal case at the time, which sparked great interest around the empire. It was where a tattoo actually saved a family's fortunes from falling into the hands of a fraudster and Ne'er-do-well (a popular term at the time, describing a person seen as a right loafer and a good-for-nothing).

In 1853 an English aristocrat by the name of Roger Tichborne, who was heir to, not only a baronetcy, but also a fortune, went missing at sea whilst on an equivalent of a gap-year (or two).

Roger had suffered a messy love affair back home and needed to escape for a while. Having the money and time to do it, he found himself in South America. However, en route from Chile to Jamaica, the ship he was sailing in was lost and assumed wrecked. News reached England many weeks later that Roger was no doubt dead. Sometime after though, rumours began circulating that the super-rich aristocrat may actually be alive and well, living in Australia. By this time, Roger's father had died and the massive inheritance, which would have been due to him, was heading in the direction of Roger's younger brother Alfred, as tradition dictates.

But before the handover of the title and assets to Alfred actually happened, the brother's mother, Lady Tichborne visited a fortune teller, who assured her that her eldest son had not perished at sea, that the rumours were correct, Roger was indeed alive and thriving in Australia! Driven by a desperate need to find her son, Lady Tichborne now firmly believing Roger was alive, took out advertisements in Australian newspapers, offering a large reward for any information leading to the discovery of her dear son, or in fact any information relating to him at all.

The advertisements worked — the power of the media came to the rescue and the results were better than anyone could have hoped. A massive amount of information came forward on Roger's whereabouts. According to dodgy claimants, looking for any sort of reward, Roger seemed to have been spotted all over Australia and on many occasions, often thousands of miles away on the same day!

A huge breakthrough came though when astonishingly, Roger Tichborne himself appeared in 1865, twelve years after his disappearance!

No one knew at the time, but 'Roger' was actually a chap called Thomas Castro, a bankrupt butcher from Wagga Wagga in New South Wales!

Lady Tichborne however was delighted beyond belief... she'd found her son, but she was no doubt surprised when she finally met the claimant. His memory of her and his previous life was sketchy to say the least and her memory of him, especially his appearance didn't quite match the view in front of her! But, nevertheless, all of this was put down to his terrible experience at sea, his near drowning, many years of hard living and post-traumatic stress! The ex-butcher from Wagga Wagga was welcomed into the family's country estate as her long-lost son 'Roger'!

Just to keep him going and because he was a bit short of

cash, the new Roger was given an annual allowance from Lady T of around £130,000 in today's terms, while his title and inheritance were sorted out!

But other members of the Tichborne family were highly sceptical about Roger and in fact, they didn't believe a word he said. This, they knew was not the same young fellow that had left the family home bound for South America. Admittedly, it had been a dozen years since, but Roger had gained a lot of weight in that time, which seemed to have changed his appearance somewhat. His manners had deteriorated quite dramatically too, and he'd developed a gruff and unsophisticated accent and general demeanour. This really wasn't like the Roger they all remembered… to those people who believed his claim though, all of this was simply put down to him spending such a long time in the colonies!

News of Roger's discovery hit the newspapers and made headlines, gripping the whole of the English-speaking world. The public were cheering on for 'Roger' even though news began circulating that many other people, not just in the Tichborne family were doubting the authenticity of the claim.

The story just kept getting juicier and juicier as supporters of 'Roger' came out of the woodwork. His former batman in the army swore it was him, as did a former slave, he'd befriended on the Duke of Buckingham's plantation in Jamaica, as well as several impoverished distant relatives… all of whom were probably hoping for a windfall once the inheritance came through!

The 'new Roger' was in-line for a fortune and Lady Tichborne was ready to hand it over to him. Eventually though a court case was brought against the butcher from Wagga Wagga by nonbelievers of his story and after several years of wrangling and twists and turns, much to the delight of the newspaper reading public, it was a tattoo (or lack of it) that ended the claim for Thomas Castro, posing as Roger Tichborne.

Well into the court case, an old friend of Roger Tichborne's turned up out of the blue to give evidence and tell a tale… and what a tale he had! The old friend was Lord Bellew, he'd been at school with Tichborne and he swore that Roger had about his person some distinctive tattoos, one of which, Lord Bellow himself had added to by tattooing the initials RCT with his very own hand onto Roger's skin! Whether Lady Tichborne knew of her son's school tattoos, we don't know, but with Lord Bellow being an honourable and upstanding member of the aristocracy, his story was obviously believed. The 'new Roger' was thoroughly checked, and it was discovered he had no tattoos, let alone one with Roger's initials… Thomas Castro, the butcher from Wagga Wagga in the colonies was convicted of perjury, sentenced to a long period in jail and the Tichborne fortune was saved by a non-existent tattoo!

Women of the empire didn't just sit back and watch as the fashion for tattoos took off either. The upper-class ladies, who partook in elegant tea parties in refined company, were known to invite along to these soirées, professional tattoo artists who would decorate hidden parts of the ladies' bodies with their newly invented electric tattoo machines. For a woman of the time, having a tattoo, even if it was always to be disguised from view and beneath layers of Victorian modesty clothing, was seen and felt as a feminist gesture. All sorts of designs and shapes were emblazoned on the bodies of these delicate, feminine and sweet creatures (the image they were expected to portray)! Even tattoos in the shape of ships anchors entwined with snakes — the kind of thing you'd expect to see on the forearm of an old white bearded seadog, were not unusual for a lady at the time! There were many instances too, where ladies had the inscriptions on their wedding rings tattooed onto their fingers beneath the rings themselves... these were particularly popular as they could easily be shown surreptitiously to a confidant over tea and cakes! And those ladies that lunched, who kept pace with modern times, and at the dawn of motoring, often had an illustration of a smart 'horseless carriage' adorned somewhere on their bodies! Feminism was really beginning to take a hold, and this was one way a lady could show to those she shared the secret of the tattoo with, that she was taking control of her life and that she wanted full control of it, including the right to vote... female fashion tattoos arrived just before the Suffragettes!

A fashionable Motor Car tattoo'

So, at the height of the British Empire, you could say that tattooing was fashionable and bang on trend with the lower classes (homemade jobs or in back rooms of smoky taverns) and the upper classes (posh tattoo parlours and travelling artists with electric machines).

Winston Churchill's mother had a snake tattooed on her wrist. Churchill himself had an anchor on his arm and it was rumoured that even Queen Victoria had one!

Oddly, it seems that the British Empire's middle classes generally rejected tattooing, thinking it positively uncouth! Today, in the 21st century, tattooing knows no class barriers, everybody's at it. It's actually becoming rarer not to have a tattoo, than to have one and here's something I bet you didn't know… there are more women in the world today with tattoos than men with tattoos… girl power!

Radioactive Make-Up

Radium was discovered by Marie Curie and her husband in 1898. Marie Curie was a well-known scientist in her day. A physicist and a chemist, who gained worldwide fame and recognition for her work, contributing to the fight against cancer. Hence the charitable organisation we all know of today.

The term 'radiation' comes from the discovery of Radium. A chemical element, which it was discovered, could help in the cure for cancer.

Many people believed that Radium was a wonder product. A magical substance that could cure just about anything. Under certain conditions, it also gave off a glorious green glow, as if it was something that had been transported to earth from another planet and so it quickly developed a mystical unearthly healing reputation.

It didn't take long then for the make-up industry to begin looking at this new space age ingredient and wondrous claims came thick and fast, once the cosmetics industry began adding Radium to its beauty products. From the early 1900s 'radioactive' make-up hit the market in a huge way. Face creams that instantly cured wrinkles, removed fat and took years off the user in a moment were all the rage. Powders, rouges, lipsticks, toothpastes and even a face powder which apparently prevented herpes, were all available on the high street, or by mail order… all of these products contained Radium and the advertisers ruthlessly used descriptions of the chemical's remarkable, almost biblical powers in their marketing. Out of interest Radium is over one million times as radioactive as Uranium. Uranium was the chemical used to make the Hiroshima bomb!

London-based cosmetics firm Radior advertised its beauty products with the great strap line *'An ever-flowing fountain of youth and beauty has at last been found in the energy rays of Radium'*… the public bought into the energy rays and everlasting beauty idea in a very big way indeed!

Radior supplied its radioactive cosmetics to Boots, the high street retailer. All five hundred and eighty stores stocked the products, as did the world-famous Harrods in Knightsbridge, as well as retailers across the empire from India to South Africa.

Worse than face creams though, was a tablet made with Radium. This one-a-day pill promised, *'a first-rate product for the intimate daily hygiene of women. Something which helps with vitality and protects against microbial infections'.* The tablet was described as being *'absolutely harmless'*!

Radium was also injected directly into the blood stream. Practitioners promised it would cure everything from hair loss to gout, high blood pressure to impotence. And because it was believed to have such a vitalising effect on the human body, Radium was even added to a wide range of commercial products from chocolates for health and wellbeing, to condoms for some apparent added boost!

Some people even drank Radium! An energy drink was marketed under the name *'Radithor'* This, in a way was the equivalent to today's many energy drinks on the market. The modern pick-me-up energy drink though, will give you a boost with a quick shot of caffeine, with little danger, to keep you working, training, or awake, whereas '*Radithor*' with its special ingredients, could have some unfortunate side effects!

The makers advertised quite astonishingly that this new invented drink was '*A cure for the Living Dead*' and that it could rejuvenate parts other drinks simply couldn't reach... it kick-started your muscles apparently and helped cure all sorts of ailments from diabetes to lack of sexual interest! The founder of the company, William Bailey, who devised and produced the drink was a Harvard University drop out. Bailey falsely claimed to be a doctor of medicine, which was obviously illegal. However, he was a marvellous marketeer, so he needs credit for that... he convinced enough people that his drink was such a wonder product that it made him very rich indeed!

Made from distilled water, with very small amounts of dissolved Radium. If drunk in moderation, the drink was not lethal or even that detrimental to health... it also didn't have any of the benefits it claimed, but that's beside the point, and can be put down to marketing speak.

However, if drunk in great quantities, more in line with the amounts consumed by today's energy drink fans, the side effects could be nasty. Take the example of the famous American athlete and socialite at the time, Ebenezer Byers. Ebenezer came from a wealthy industrialist family. A very active chap, he was the U.S. Amateur golf champion in 1906 and had a great reputation for having an over-active libido! However, after an unfortunate fall, at speed, from a railway sleeping berth, he injured his arm quite badly. The injury caused him persistent pain and after a number of visits to his doctors, it his was suggested he drink 'Radithor' which the doctor claimed would alleviate his discomfort. William Bailey, the owner of Radithor was known to offer doctors a percentage kick back from every sale of his drink!

Ebenezer began taking dose after dose of the drink and soon became addicted to it. He'd commented that the results were fantastic, that it had toned up his muscles, helped no end with the pain and he so loved the energy it gave him. So, Radithor he claimed did him the world of good and he was a huge advocate of it. He was also a big fan of the company and its owner who produced it too. He told everyone he met about the merits of the drink. This was, no doubt, much to the delight of William Bailey!

Sadly for Ebenezer however, it was proved that the drink wasn't as good for him as he thought it was. He took gravely ill, began to lose weight, had terrible headaches and his teeth began to fall out. This was followed by terrible bone deterioration around his upper and lower jaw, and it was said that his body was disintegrating. It got worse very quickly and Ebenezer died in 1932 of 'radiation poisoning'.

This was a big media story at the time. With him being so famous, Ebenezer's death made all the newspapers and the Wall Street Journal ran with the headline '*The Radium water worked fine… until his jaw came off*'.

Ebenezer Byers was buried in a lead lined coffin for safety reasons!

What about the make-up? Luckily for the consumers of the day, due to the cosmetic manufacturers cutting corners to save money, the side effects of the make-ups were not nearly as bad as the drinks and some of the pills, with barely any evidence of any harm caused to any make-up wearers.

It seems that the cosmetic companies may have used the name and reputation of Radium to great effect in their advertising and PR, but they put very little of the chemical into their cosmetics!

Radium was highly expensive and the cosmetics industry soon worked out that there was much more money to be made by not putting very much Radium in their wonder products, than the other way around!

Some might say that the cosmetic makers of the time were being somewhat disingenuous. The public paid for expensive beauty products, because of the life-changing promises made by the industry. All of which could be attributed to the apparent high levels of Radium in their products. But it seems that all the while the make-up industry had been scamming the public, or at least leading them astray somewhat. Cosmetics firms rightly understood that people buy into promises, oddly more than results!

Ironically though, this was a scam with great side benefits... make-up users may not have been privy to the fountain of youth, as promised in the adverts, but at least they weren't being poisoned to death!

The same couldn't be said for people working, hands-on with Radium!

Radium, as well as everything else was also highly luminous. A paint was developed from the chemical called 'radio-luminescent paint' and around the turn of the 20th century, this was used heavily in the watch making industry. The newly invented paint was applied to the dials of time pieces, making the markers and the hands luminous and therefore enabling the wearer to tell the time in the dark. This was just another amazing use of the newly discovered chemical. It really was the chemical that just kept on giving!

The painted watch faces were called 'Radium Dials' and as you can imagine, the watches with the luminous faces were hugely popular and sales took off across the world. The watch dials were generally painted by young women on production lines and most of the time pieces were manufactured in America.

The Americans had been dominating the mass manufacture of watches, using the production line system for a couple of decades by now and it was cheaper for the empire to buy in these watches than make them at home, before sending them around her colonies. The British watch and clock making industry simply couldn't compete with the cheap, mass produced watches the Americans were producing and many of the British makers went out of business because of it. This was the beginning of Britain's de-industrialisation process, where she slowly but surely lost the title she had gained, at the beginning of the industrial revolution of 'Workshop of the World'.

The watch factory workers known as the 'Radium Girls' sat at their stations and painted hundreds of watch-faces each day. It was close up work and with the hands and markers being so small, it was important to make sure that the brush was not only fine and in good order, but that it had a tiny point on it, which enabled the girls to paint precisely and of course efficiently… their work itself was timed. They were expected to paint perfectly, a set number of dials per day, without any mistakes. To get a sharp and precise point to the hairs, the girls rolled the paint brushes in their mouths. Using their saliva to mould the finest point possible on the brush, before dipping it into the radio-luminescent paint. Doing this constantly throughout their shifts and over months or years caused them to digest large quantities of Radium (with obvious and disastrous consequences). But, not only did they put the radiative brushes in their mouths, they also painted themselves with the luminous paint for special nights out on the town! The Radium Girls could always be spotted in bars and clubs in the towns near the watch factories. They'd literally be glowing in the dark! The girls, whilst out enjoying themselves were known for their luminous long nails and some, even, for their luminous teeth... all covered in radiative paint!

A Radium Girl

This look certainly got them noticed, but the damage that

was being done to their heath was appalling. Soon after the luminous qualities of Radium were discovered, the workers in the watch factories began to develop all sorts of horrific conditions relating to radiation poisoning, especially around the mouth area. Jawbone degeneration, gum diseases, teeth falling out and general poor health. This way of painting was eventually banned, as was the paint itself once the medical experts discovered the hideous side effects of ingesting Radium.

As for the 'glow in the dark' watches themselves. They lost their luminous quality over time, but the ill health effects of the paint can still be felt and suffered, if you're not careful and if you own one of these early 20th century time pieces today… whether or not it's luminous!

The face dials may not be lighting up darkened rooms any longer, but don't let that fool you. There's still danger there. The radiative Radium, although no longer luminous, is still present on the watch hands and digits. You see, the chemical Radium can, remarkably, remain radioactive for hundreds of years, so great care is taken by modern watch specialists who handle and service these pieces today. Loose, flaky Radium paint is easily inhaled. Breathe it in and you could feasibly give yourself a dose of unhealthy radiation. Watch out then and be aware, these time pieces are still out there. They were made in their multi thousands, and they were sent to all parts of the old British Empire!

During the First World War, women filled the factories in place of the men, who were fighting in France. They manufactured everything from boots for the troops to bombs to blast the Germans out of their trenches. To make bombs, the women often had to work with the highly explosive material

TNT. Over time, the substance could cause lung, stomach and skin problems. The girls soon discovered though that TNT powder, when rubbed in their hair, worked as a brilliant dye… no one knew why, but TNT powder turned anyone who used it on their hair into a sexy red head. A right bomb shell… especially if the powder came into contact with a naked flame! But back to watches for a moment. If you wear an automatic self-winding watch, this might be of interest to you.

The world's first self-winder time piece was invented by John Harwood from Bolton, England. Harwood served as an armoury staff sergeant in World War I where he invented an automatic pistol and an automatic screw driver! But sometime after the war, he came up with the idea for an automatic watch that could wind itself simply through the movement the wearer made in the wrist.

The idea was sparked when he witnessed some children playing on a see-saw in the local park. The principle of the up and down momentum, he thought, if applied to a watch mechanism, could possibly keep the watch wound without having to do it manually. He was right, he invented the system, the idea was patented in 1924 and Harwood self-winders found themselves spread across the empire in their tens of thousands in no time at all. Sadly for John Harwood, the great depression bankrupted his company in 1930.

Rolex, the Great British Empire watchmaker!
If you're lucky enough to own a Rolex watch, it'll more than likely be an automatic self-winding one. Rolex took Harwood's automatic design, improved it and created their world famous 'Oyster' water proof automatic in 1931. And, when it comes to watches, Rolex, is one of the biggest, most recognised and most iconic brands in the world.

But, ask anyone where Rolex was founded and the vast majority of people will reply 'Switzerland' … but they'd be wrong. Rolex is a product of the British Empire!

Founded in London in 1905 by friends Hans Wilsdorf and Alfred Davis. The company remained in London until just after the end of World War I, when they relocated lock, stock and barrel to Geneva.

You see, the British government, due to the financial burden brought on by the Great War was effectively bankrupt.

So, after the war in 1918 in an attempt to balance the British books, the government increased taxes across the board, including duty hikes on imported high end watch parts, which Rolex, to make their sought-after watches, were importing from Switzerland.

Production costs then for the Rolex Watch Company in London immediately increased due to the new import taxes. These extra costs were difficult to pass onto their customers because of the economic devastation caused by the war and the obvious decline in consumer spending power because of it. Not a good situation for any company to find itself in.

Luckily though for Rolex, they became a target for the Swiss!

Rolex had gained an enviable reputation within the watch industry.

A British company, based in London, but Switzerland wanted them!

And you've got to give the Swiss some credit here. They saw an opportunity to tempt Rolex to relocate their operation from financially ruined Britain to Switzerland. So, with some enticing Swiss tax breaks on offer, plus no import duties to pay, the temptation to save a load of cash was just too great… Rolex decamped to Geneva in 1919!

How about some great empire inventions

Spa treatments and home rocking baths

Hydrotherapy became popular during the 1800s. Water treatment for good health was thought to be a natural and spiritual method of maintaining a balanced body and mind. Spiritualism itself blossomed too around the same time and I'll get to that later, but hydropathy as it was called then was all the rage.

The general idea behind hydropathy was to encourage what they called a 'crisis' in or on the body. Not something you'd imagine you'd want to encourage, but nevertheless, a good 'crisis' when it came to water therapy was seen as a very good thing indeed.

Water, especially swishing, moving and splashing water was believed to cleanse and flush any impurities out of the body.

Rapidly moving water, they said at the time, was able to invade any cracks, wounds and imperfections in the skin. These areas, it was believed were full of impure fluids, which needed to be decontaminated... and splashing about in water was the thing that would decontaminate you!

A really quite superb invention, designed especially for home use, hit the market in the 1890s. It was a bath that was designed a little like a rocking chair and so it rocked forwards and backwards and it was truly cutting-edge stuff. Admittedly, you'd need to do the rocking yourself, but nevertheless, it was indeed a rocking bath and it didn't half splash water around! This is exactly what everyone needed at home to encourage and maintain good physical and mental health. The clever contraption was marketed under a number of product names, like 'The Nautilus' and 'The Niagara'. The makers guaranteed that the rocking baths would keep your blood in active circulation (which, by all accounts is vital to life) so that was a great selling slogan! They promised that the experience would make you believe that you were not actually at home, in the living room or on the kitchen floor rocking around in a tin bath. No, you'd be transported in your mind to the glorious seaside, where you'd bathe in the wild sea, with waves lapping over your head. Some promised the feeling of a real rushing river each time you jumped into the tin tub... yes, you'd receive 'a treat never experienced before'... and to top it all, you only needed three buckets of hot or cold water to get the whole contraption going. And amazingly, after all this rocking, rolling and splashing around, the adverts promised that absolutely no water whatsoever would spill onto your floor at home (the Trades Description Act didn't come in until 1968)!

This health-giving bathtub, was a seriously good invention and it sold well, and particularly well in America... the rocking bath was the perfect invention to thoroughly cleanse your body of all its nasties. And if you were moving to any of the many colonies around the empire, you could easily transport one with you too. And wherever you ended up, the bush, the jungle, the outback, or the wilderness, you could, each time you hopped into the rocking bath, close your eyes and imagine that you were bathing in the freezing sea at

Blackpool, whilst enjoying yourself in your rocking bath!

And to do this, all you needed to do was pour the three buckets of water into the rocking bath, hop in, grab hold of the handle above your head and rock as wildly as you could. This, it was promised would cause the much desired 'crisis'… and hopefully the right sort of crisis!

A Rocking Bath

The water then rushed into all the cracks and crevices in the body and did its super cleaning job. Simply splashing around on the living room floor, no soap needed, was all that was required.

All of the cracks, creases and horrid folds in your skin would be, customers were told, filled with pure, healing, soothing water and the unwanted puss (as they described it at the time) that was hiding there, unseen, would be flushed out into the water.

So, once the body was cleansed, you'd jump out of the tin apparatus refreshed, decontaminated of puss and rejuvenated… basically, feeling fabulous.

The now foul water would of course need to be disposed

of and you wouldn't forget to give the tub a good rub down, ready for the next occupant!

The rocking bathtub was a fashionable home health treatment, but other procedures were available too, especially in the fashionable spa towns around Britain. This is where the health practitioners purged the paying patients' bodies of puss with hot steam to sweat it out, ice cold water to shock it out (plunge pools) and odd shaped baths in which to sit uncomfortably upright in for long periods of time… there were also special baths designed just for the head and a number of types of douche baths, designed specifically for the unmentionable areas! The way forward at the time, was with water, as it seemed to cure most things. You could also drink it of course and this was encouraged. The foul smelling and tasting spa waters which made most people vomit, were guzzled by the gallon!

Hydropathy became quite accepted as a genuine medical treatment for all sorts of ailments and appealed to people from all classes, if they could afford it.

Compared to some methods of health treatment, the water system seemed so much easier and more personal (especially with some of the baths!) and less complicated, without the use of any of the scientific and medical language used by traditional and often snooty doctors. These doctors were often accused of confusing people intentionally with their flowery talk… and then charging them mightily for the privilege, without ever curing them of an illness!

Hydropathy was actually a return to the ancient ways of nature and was first rediscovered in the 18th century when the English physician Sir John Floyer became fascinated by local peasants whom he witnessed and observed at length bathing in the local cold spring waters.

Sir John discovered that the country folk used the waters not only for cleansing, but also for health reasons. They believed, as they told him, like their ancestors did before them, in the healing powers of the water.

Much research later and Sir John published a book on the subject of healing waters. It was a success and was reprinted several times throughout the 18th and 19th centuries.

So, this being the time of the empire and the industrial revolution, the old ways of our ancestors were indeed industrialised and healthy amazing spa towns around Britain sprang up from the 18th century onwards. These towns and their treatments were much employed and needed, not only by permanent residents of Britain, but by worn out and exhausted returning colonials, mainly from hot and sultry India.

Yes, running the empire at the coal face was a rough job and the British-Indian families who retired back to the old country were often in need of some rest, recuperation and rejuvenation, after spending so much time in what was believed to be the unhealthy climate of the tropics.

This process of recovery often started at one of the many spa towns. Cheltenham became a particularly popular destination for the Anglo-Indians. The reason Cheltenham was doing so much business was down to brilliant marketing. It seems that physicians and journalists, along with adverts taken out in Indian newspapers were constantly recommending Cheltenham as 'the place to go' for anyone, who on returning to Britain needed curing of the 'Bodily consequences of colonial life'!

The most common consequences for people living in an unhealthy climate were liver and spleen problems, malaria, anaemia and 'disorders of young females'… best not to ask!

Obviously, the climate and conditions in the tropics were not particularly well suited to the delicate British constitution or make-up. However, the climate alone could not be blamed for all the ailments the colonials carried home with them.

People at the time also commented on the 'Consequences of a debouched colonial lifestyle'! Heavy drinking, parties, too much spicy food and cavorting with all and sundry could and did lead to all sorts of ailments. It was said that 'what goes on in the tropics, stays in the tropics' which is all well and good, but sadly, often, what went on in the tropics was brought home in the form of one uncomfortable sickness or terrible infection or another!

Some of the returning colonials were not very popular back home in Britain, especially if they arrived back looking like they'd made lots of money. These were more often than not high-ranking officials working for The East India Company, or merchants, businesspeople, or worst of all, the wheeler dealers in one trade or another who'd left old Blighty with no money and in rags, only to return years later, positively dripping in cash. Jealousy of course played a part, but these worldly travellers with all their wealth and flashy ways were the oligarchs of their day and with all their spending power too… and about as popular! They were seen as being quite uncouth (envy again, I think) and accusations and rumours spread about how they'd more than likely made their money by foul means, through corrupt trade or practises. This group of 'nouveau riche' colonials were referred to as 'Nabob' by those that wished to give insult to them. The term was meant to be an affront and was taken from the Hindi language in which it related to the over-paid governors of the old Mughal

Empire… who were, in their day about as popular as the returning British Nabob's!

British-Indian Nabob families, with all their hard cash, bought up companies in Britain, country estates and often went into politics too. They had the money to do what they liked and because of this, most people were green with envy and absolutely hated them!

How many returning 'Nabob's' were truly hurt by the insults thrown at them back home in old Blighty, who can tell. However, I'm quite sure, they were probably quite pleased to be rich enough to be referred to as a 'Nabob'! And on their return, after their years of colonial adventures, suffering in the warm tropical climate and making stacks of cash, there were plenty of Nabob's who needed to go into 'water rehab' in Cheltenham!

The first mass produced 'Toothbrush'

In 1770, an Englishman called William Addis was sitting in prison one day (he was there for causing a riot in London) with nothing really to do and found himself observing someone using a broom to sweep the filthy prison floor. Watching the bristles pick up and scrub away the dirt from the damp stones, gave him the brilliant idea for a toothbrush! He imagined the same principle as the broom but miniaturised for the mouth. The method to clean teeth at the time was generally with a cloth, some soot from the fire, a bit of spit and to add a little grit, some salt, or if you were lucky, finely crushed seashells. If you didn't have these ingredients, then, a twig would have to do, or even the sharp end of a bird's feather to pick out any stuck bits!

William realised that it was high time this old method of tooth hygiene was modernised. So, after his next meal containing meat, he saved a suitably sized length of bone and obtained some pig bristles from a friendly prison guard. William, then whittled away at the bone, shaping it perfectly to fit in the hand comfortably. He drilled tiny holes in the bone for the bristles to go through, fitted them, tied them off and sealed them in place with drops of animal fat glue. This implement, made in prison was William Addis' first ever manufactured toothbrush.

When he left prison, he soon set up in business making his

design of toothbrush and they sold like 'hot cakes' (a mid-19th century saying, describing cheap hot pancakes, that sell very quickly. It is from the period of British Empire... although it originated in America).

William couldn't make the toothbrushes fast enough. He hit the big time and he became very rich, very quickly. He died in 1808 and left the company to his son, also called William and the company continued to flourish, making stacks of toothbrushes and stacks of cash!

Oral health, as a rule was pretty diabolical at this time, but the toothbrush was a game changer. Simple, effective and inexpensive, the new design transformed the lives of hundreds of thousands of people. The simple brushing removed plaque, prevented cavities and even stimulated the gums, helping stave off gum disease. But, best of all, the toothbrush saved many an excruciating trip to the Victorian dentist, or agonising tooth ache in the tropics.

The firm, which is still trading today, amazingly stayed in the same family hands, making toothbrushes in England right up to 1996, when the family sold the firm to a management buyout.

Under the name Wisdom Toothbrushes, the company have been in the toothbrush business for over two hundred years and today, they make around seventy million toothbrushes a year!

The Modern Bicycle

Bicycles of sorts had been around since the early 19th century — originally called a 'Dandy Horse' or a 'Hobby Horse' and they were strange vehicles indeed. No pedals, no brakes or suspension. The rider sat astride the heavy wooden contraption and pushed themselves along with their feet and occasionally free wheeled when enough momentum was built up, or when the rider pointed the thing down a hill… stopping under emergency conditions was impossible and many an accident was witnesses by much bemused and equally amused and afraid pedestrians!

The first official recorded traffic offence involving such a contraption was reported in a Glasgow newspaper in 1842. The newspaper informed the interested readers that an anonymous gentleman from Dumfriesshire was fined five shillings for running a pedestrian over whilst astride a Velocipede of ingenious design (Velocipede: A human powered land machine, with one or more wheels).

Velocipedes of all designs were thought of as dangerous, not only for the riders, but for anyone within fifty yards of the machine!

Inventors didn't give up on the general idea of the design though and improvements kept on coming, with the eventual introduction of pedals and the invention in the 1870s of the famous 'Penny Farthing' Also known as a 'High Wheeler'. This was the first two wheeled form of transport known also as a 'Bicycle'. Its design, with a massive front wheel (Penny) and the tiny rear wheel (Farthing) provided the dare devil rider, who effectively sat on top of the front wheel with a far greater speed (due to the size of the front wheel) and long-distance touring ability. The huge front wheel, with a thin solid rubber tyre, also helped with shock absorption, but it still jarred and shook the rider's bones and caused no end of terrible injury when the rider was thrown over the handlebars from a great height... called 'taking a header'. And because the pedals were attached solidly to the centre of the massive front wheel, this meant that the rider, when free wheeling needed to keep their feet well away from the insanely fast spinning pedals, as they'd be turning as quickly as the wheel itself. Make a simple mistake here and a spinning pedal could easily break an ankle... and many ankles were broken! The pedals also acted as the machine's braking system. Pushing backwards on the pedals was the only way to slow the thing down. This was impossible of course if the rider was travelling at speed, freewheeling, with the pedals spinning madly down a hill. So, if a sudden obstruction, like a horse and cart, a cow, or a pedestrian appeared in the middle of the road, the consequences could be catastrophic for all involved... especially for the rider, who was sat five feet in the air and was often catapulted great distances head first!

A Penny Farthing

You can understand then, why Penny Farthings were generally thought of as being too dangerous for everyday use, for most ordinary people. They were popular though with young and reckless riders, who set up bicycle clubs around the country, race meetings and long-distance tours. These monster size machines were such an unusual sight though in rural towns and villages, that locals lined the streets if they heard there was a tour coming through… they'd cheer as the heroic riders tore past them at great speed… and all the while, the spectators would be hoping to witness one dramatic crash or another. Penny Farthings had this reputation and spectators loved them!

Penny Farthings were a short-lived fad though, they were soon out of fashion and out-invented with far better designs, but you can credit them and their brave, pioneering riders with the invention of cycling as a popular sport.

And talking of pioneers and adventurers, the very first person to ride a bike around the world was an eccentric Englishman, Thomas Stevens, who after moving to America, set off from San Francisco in April 1884 on his 'Penny Farthing'. He travelled light, packing just a small handlebar bag, containing socks, a spare shirt, a raincoat (which when required, doubled up as a tent), a bedroll and a pocket revolver! He started his epic journey by cycling three thousand seven hundred miles to Boston on the east coast of America. This first leg took him just over three months, by which time he was described by witnesses as being as tanned as a nut!

Thomas gave talks along the route to local cycle clubs and by all accounts, he kept the crowds entertained with his stories of adventures seen from the height of his 'High Wheeler' as he crossed America. He told tales of Indians, mountain passes, storms and terrible dangers on the road.

Next, he sailed to England, where he set off again on his machine from Liverpool. And because, by now, he was becoming something of a celebrity with newspapers on both sides of the Atlantic covering his epic journey, crowds amassed in the city to wave him off.

He rode through England, sensibly wearing a helmet (an old military version, painted white) and crossed the channel into France. On through Germany, Austria, Hungary and all the way to Constantinople, where he rested for a while, carried out some maintenance on his bike and shared stories of America and his travels so far with locals and interpreters who couldn't get enough of his adventurous tales. Setting off again, he found his way to Teheran, where he stayed a while as the guest of the Shah of Iran, who was obviously intrigued by the strange Englishman.

Afghanistan caused Thomas a few problems. He was arrested there, but was well treated by his guards who were fascinated by him and amazed by his demonstrations and tricks performed on his Penny Farthing! He was instructed to leave the country and when the armed Afghans escorted him out of their territory, with him being much faster on his bike than they were on foot and mules, they allowed him to cycle ahead of them, as long as he waited every now and again for them to catch up. Such was the speed of his machine though, the Afghans became nervous that he might decide to abscond into the country, where he really wasn't welcome and they may not be able to catch him! So, they decided to dismantle the bike and strap it to a packhorse for the rest of the journey to the border! The rough packing caused some damage to his spokes though, but these were repaired just beyond the border by local tribal gunsmiths, who drilled new holes into the rims, made and fitted new spikes... and sent Thomas back off, on the road again!

Once in India, he rode along the famous Grand Trunk Road, which, although it was at least two thousand five hundred years old already, had in recent years been rebuilt by the British to help them move trade goods and supplies through Asia. The road was over two thousand miles long, it's still in use today and Thomas commented that it offered some 'excellent wheeling' which allowed him to travel with great haste across India.

From Calcutta, he caught the steamer to Hong Kong and from there, he rode into Eastern China, where he needed to take refuge from some locals who were rioting against the French... with obvious language difficulties and similar appearance, he didn't want to be mistaken for a Frenchman!

From there, another steamer took Thomas to Japan, where he said he was delighted and enamoured by Japanese culture and the calmness of its people. Once, finally through Japan, he boarded a boat bound for San Francisco and arrived back on the west coast of America in December 1886 after two and a half years cycling around the world. The first person ever to do it.

Around the same time as Thomas Stevens' epic adventure on his High Wheeler, the 1880s saw a new design of bicycle developed and one that resembles the bikes we know and love today.

Chain driven machines hit the market, with brakes and with gears too, so there was no need any longer to have such a massive 'Penny Farthing' type wheel at the front to build up speed. Bicycles then became low to the ground, far safer and speed could be increased by clicking through to a higher gear. Another new design was the pneumatic tyre, developed by Scotsman John Boyd Dunlop. The cushioned, air-filled rubber band, separated the rider from the harsh and bumpy cobbled roads and pothole filled lanes.

This leap in bicycle design was the equivalent to the transition from propeller driven aircraft to jet power. Cycling was now suddenly opened up to a mass market. This new and modern form of transportation became known as the 'Safety Bicycle' and the overall appearance is really no different to a bike of today. It was English inventors and engineers who get the credit for bringing this new design to life. In 1885 John Kemp Starley, launched into the market his own version of the Safety Bicycle known as the 'Rover' and it proved to be a big hit with the public.

A Safety Bicycle

A new dawn in transportation had arrived and 'Rover' bicycles found their way into the daily lives of thousands of Britons —

and for the very first time, bicycles were now being ridden by everyone, men, women and all ages, not just young men full of bravado on their 'High Wheelers'!

Not long after, in 1888 The Raleigh Cycle Company was founded to make their own version of Safety Bicycles and soon, they became the biggest bicycle manufacturer in the world. Based in Nottingham, England, Raleigh bikes made their way right across the British Empire, where they had an enormous and beneficial effect on all levels of society... and still do.

Advertisements for the new safety bikes told stories and showed images of men being chased by Lions in Africa... but luckily for them, due to the colonial having a safety bicycle shipped out to them, they escaped with their lives. This was put down to the speed and agility of the new safety bicycle!

A Safety Bicycle at Work!

Back in Britain, it wasn't all sweetness and light though. Bicycles, and more particularly their riders, were gaining a terrible reputation in the 1890s for unruly behaviour on their bikes... accused of cutting up horses, riding in front of carriages, not adhering to road instructions in the forms of signs, especially 'Stop' signs and generally not being responsible in charge of such fast machines!

The police of course on foot could never catch a misbehaving cyclist... but not for long. The police force were soon supplying their constables with fleets of safety cycles, and from the 1880s onwards, Bobbies on bikes were a common sight. In the mid-20th century however, things began to change. Patrolling policemen were more likely to be seen in 'Panda Cars'. The Panda Car as a matter of interest, gets its name from an unusual source. The police cars were painted in pale blue with white door and roof panels, but with popular police shows on TV like 'Z Cars' in the 1960s and 1970s, the police vehicles were seen tearing around the streets of Britain in black and white vision... the vast majority of the population did not own a colour TV. Therefore, the blue and white panels, showed up on the millions of tellies around the country as dark grey and light grey... not quite black and white like a Panda, but the nickname was coined, and it stuck!

Now in the 21st century there is a renewed interest in police bicycles. They're obviously greener and far more practical in our busy and overcrowded cities and so they are once again a common site.

Today there are over one billion bicycles in use. They far exceed the number of cars in the world and bikes are still the principal mode of transport for thousands of communities around the globe... and they're getting even more popular in the 21st century.

Out of interest, the best-selling bicycle ever made, is the Chinese model known as the 'Flying Pigeon'… well over five hundred million have been produced so far!

The birth of 'Gorilla' marketing

Advertising during the latter part of the 19th century and at the height of the British Empire started to develop a more sophisticated, targeted and cunning approach. Consumers were getting mightily fed up with huge advertising hoardings, constantly pushing advertisements as they went about their daily business. Look at old photos of the period and you'll see enamel signs, posters and banners everywhere. They're hung from every available gable-end of buildings, shop fronts are covered in them, they're on the side of omnibuses, as well as trams and advertisements are littered throughout every newspaper. Almost every one of these adverts claimed one amazing health cure or another, something delicious to eat (and often not) or wonder beauty products, claiming life changing results, that usually had no beneficial results at all… and sometimes the reverse!

Consumers then were rapidly becoming blind to the bombardment of adverts.

The buying public were not only fed up with the number of ads they were being subjected too, but they were also wise to the mass marketing and generally, they were taking no notice of the sales pitches, coming at them from all angles… there was too much information flying around. A lot of it was known to be fraudulent, or at least misleading and people simply became oblivious to the marketing and generally ignored most of it. Not dissimilar to you browsing the internet today, with your screen constantly popping up adverts. You, no doubt, on autopilot, simply click them off without taking any notice of what the adverts are trying to sell you. The same thing was happening with hoardings, posters and press advertisements… increasingly, the ads were just getting ignored by the passers-by, who were of course the target market, the spending public… and the advertising agencies knew it.

Something new was needed then. A fresh approach to selling was required and iconic products began taking more adventurous and audacious steps with their marketing… They began 'thinking outside of the box', as a more modern advertising executive might say!

Beecham's the British pharmaceutical company, who'd been in business making medicinal powders and pills for around a hundred years at the time, were looking for new ways to interact with the public. Interacting, with the sole intention, of course, of selling them more of their products and beating off the competition!

So, with the traditional billboards losing their appeal, Beecham's advertising gurus experimented with new ways of getting their message out there to the people. This was in a rush to beat any competitors to their pounds, shillings and pence.

As an example, rather than paying to advertise on the side of a building, or a tram, Beecham's ran a freebie campaign. They had no intention of handing out free headache powders, they wanted to sell those, so what they did was begin producing and giving away free sails for leisure boats! Boating was an incredibly popular pastime and if you owned a boat, small or large, if it had sails, then Beecham's offered to give you 'free gratis' nice new ones to fit to your boat and to give it a new lease of life... as we know nothing in marketing and promotion is really ever free, so the sails themselves were plastered with Beecham's company logos and the leisure boaters became part of the Beecham's marketing team (unpaid)!

Boating was popular, not only with the sailors themselves, but also with spectators. The public loved to spend time watching sailing boats. Visitors then, on day trips away, whether to a boating lake, or to the seaside, would see lovely, privately owned yachts, small and large, bobbing about in the water... and most of them advertising Beecham's products on their brand new and fabulous sails!

This was the beginning of what we call today 'gorilla' marketing. Gorilla marketing is all about taking the customer by surprise, hijacking their emotions and feelings to send them a message about a certain product… and doing all of these things without the potential customer actually knowing the trick is being played on them, is even better!

What Beecham's did was really quite innovative — rather than relying on the potential buyer stopping and reading an advertising board, which people had generally stopped doing, Beecham's sent floating billboards right past and in front of their captive audiences' eyes… and the audience couldn't keep their eyes of the advertisements!

The buying public were sat by the side of touristy lakes, or on beaches, having fun, eating picnics, feeling relaxed and at ease… all the while, watching the lovely sight of sailing boats passing by. Waving at the sailors, shouting hellos, and generally having a jolly good time. But little did they know, Beecham's were hitting the day trippers hard with their gorilla marketing! The idea behind the cunning plan was to impregnate the name 'Beecham' into the minds of their potential customers, without the customers feeling like they'd been forced into it and sold too. Then, sometime later, the customer, the marketeers gambled, would walk into a chemist shop, feeling ill, looking for some sort of remedial medicine. They'd then see a Beecham's product prominently displayed and not only would the name now be instantly recognisable, but the image of it, the marketeers hoped would conjure up in the customers mind, happy memories of feeling healthy and chirpy. Thoughts of lovely warm, carefree day trips away, watching boats sail by. So, instantly comforted by these memories, the customer would, no doubt, decide to buy Beecham's!

Gorilla marketing worked. It was clever stuff. And there were even unexpected marketing opportunities that came along too, including with the boat sail give-away.

On one occasion, a 'Beecham boat' went to the heroic rescue of two people who were in danger of drowning, just off the coast. The amateur sailors with their beautiful new and free Beecham's sails, saved the lives of the two swimmers and the story made it into the local newspaper. Naturally, Beecham's PR machine, once they heard about the rescue, went into overdrive and pushed the story out there as many newspapers around the country as possible. The press release to the media mentioned that it was a 'Beecham's' sponsored boat that was responsible for the rescue. Another example of cute gorilla marketing and suggestion. Reading the story in the papers, you might get the impressions that Beecham's themselves had a hand in the rescue!

Bovril

But it was another British firm that took this new form of marketing to an altogether new level. You might be surprised to hear that Bovril, that iconic British institution, known for its delicious beefy hot drink, was, in the late Victorian period, partly responsible for the success of the British Army during the Boer Wars in South Africa… or so it was advertised and marketed at the time!

The British fought two wars with the mainly Dutch descended Boers in South Africa. The first being in 1880 and the second from 1899 to 1902 and this, the second Boer War was the one Bovril particularly used as a brilliant marketing tool to sell its superfood and super powered 'Beef Tea'!

Bovril boasted and advertised widely that it supplied the British Army in South Africa with eighty-five thousand pounds of its product and hundreds of thousands of emergency rations containing Bovril to the British troops. This, the marketing suggested was to revive the weary troops.

And apparently, it didn't just revive them either? Bovril gave them muscles, super strength and super energy to keep them fighting day and night... yes, the easy to make anywhere drink prepared the British lads for battle. And accordingly, it also aided their recovery once they'd been shot or blown up! Even catching an awful disease wasn't much of a problem... just put the kettle on and have a mug of Bovril! Bovril was winning the war for the British!

The second Boer War became the first conflict in history to be a public media event. Not only were newspapers carrying the tales of action, but the new 'electric theatres' were showing amazing, real moving film footage of the British soldiers carrying out daring and valiant attacks against the enemy, the Boer... most of the action was actually filmed using jobbing actors on Hampstead Heath in London, but no one knew that at the time. This was a form of 'Gorilla Propaganda' on behalf of the government. Keeping British spirts up back at home was vital to the war effort and to maintain public support for the fighting.

A new type of advert was also taken out called an 'advertorial' which was effectively what looked like an editorial piece in a newspaper, seemingly written by a journalist and reporting on the facts of a story, but in actual fact, the piece was written by the marketing department at Bovril!

Bovril produced drawings of weary and worn-out British soldiers in South Africa, looking down at heart and sad to be such a long way from home. That was the picture of the poor chaps before they'd been given a drink of Bovril though. This was followed by a second picture of the same soldiers, moments after having a good mug of Bovril. In this one, the lads, miraculously now looked bright eyed, re-energised, plumped up, powerful, strong and fully restored to health and fitness, ready to go into battle again on behalf of you, of Britain and for the empire... crikey, what a product!

Bovril jumped into celebrity endorsements too. Footballers, actors, famous log rollers (a popular spectator sport at the time) even royalty. (They used Queen Victoria in their advertising without her permission!) And one marketing campaign included an image of the current Pope at the time, Pope Leo XIII. Leo was shown on posters and in newspapers all over the Empire. He was sitting on his throne, adorned in full Papal regalia... whilst holding a very large mug of Bovril! Along with the image, showing God's representative on earth enjoying a Bovril, the advert had a slogan, emblazoned across it, which read *'The two infallible powers — The Pope & Bovril'* ... You couldn't really get a higher endorsement than that of the Pope... the message sent by the poster was, if the Pope drank Bovril, then, surely you should too? In true gorilla marketing fashion, Bovril never actually asked the Pope whether he drank Bovril or not, or even asked him for his permission to use his image in the advert... you've got to love their style!

Many well-known people of the time were approached to endorse Bovril. Eugene Sandow was a famous strongman of the day and he claimed that it was Bovril that gave him his strength! Ernest Shackleton, the Antarctic explorer loved his 'beef tea' and when talking about his latest expedition and what he might be taking with him, he was quoted as saying 'It has to be Bovril'

Bovril was endorsed by scientists, dieticians and doctors who claimed the delicious meaty drink could even cure the flu. Bovril was liquid life they suggested and in fact, it was said that Bovril could supply everything short of 'everlasting youth' and 'the power to raise the dead'!

When it came to the war in South Africa, Bovril didn't only keep the fighting troopers in tip top condition, the company also kept the public back home in Britain informed and up to date with all the most recent news and action stories. The company called it the 'Bovril War Cable Scheme' and it was a supremely successful advertising campaign, which kept Bovril in its customers' minds.

The company set up thousands of what they called 'Bovril Boards' in grocers, newsagent and convenience stores right across Britain. When war news broke, the latest updates were pinned onto the Bovril Boards for all to read. Bovril, you see, had access to the 'All Red Line' which was the telegraph system that connected the empire. This is how the latest news reached Britain from South Africa almost instantaneously. The updated news was then quickly sent, again by telegraph, around the country to be picked up, written out and immediately transported to local shops by uniformed Bovril messengers, whose job it was to pin the news onto the boards. Their transportation was of course, the all new and super-fast Safety Cycles!

So, to get the most up to date war news, rather than waiting for the newspapers to be printed and delivered the following day, you could always nip to your local shop and check out the in-store 'Bovril Board'. Here, the news boards informed you as to exactly what was going on and almost in real time. It was effectively an early version of 'rolling news' and that news might only be a few hours old, which was remarkable for the time. People congregated around the boards in the shops and discussed the latest broadcasts from the front. And all the while, Bovril was there, quietly 'gorilla marketing' itself to you! Almost subliminally, the Bovril marketing team, sent your brain messages that the beefy tea was not only good for your health and was looking after the boys at the front, but that it was dependable, reliable and patriotic. A damned good British product to be proud of... all of which might encourage you to pick up a jar while you were in the shop!

Alternatively, if you didn't fancy the effort of trekking to your local convenience store several times a day for updates, you could, for a small fee have the latest news from Africa delivered to your door, personally, by a Bovril messenger. Not dissimilar to signing up to news alerts on your mobile phone today. But rather than your phone pinging an alert, you'd have a knock at the door by a Bovril representative, who'd relay the latest reports!

The founder of Bovril, a Scotsman John Lawson Johnston, lived just outside London in a very large and impressive house, locally and fondly referred to as 'Bovril Castle'.

Around the turn of the 20th century, Johnston sold Bovril for two million pounds (around two hundred and seventy million in today's terms) and then spent his time between England and France. He died in Cannes aboard his rather palatial yacht named the 'White Ladye'... many people at the time were surprised to hear that his boat wasn't called 'Bovril'!

The very first postage stamp in the world — The Penny Black

The stamp that every collector knows of, and every proper stamp collection has, was the world's very first postal stamp, and it changed postal systems around the globe forever and for the better.

Introduced in 1840 in the early years of Queen Victoria's reign and for use within the British Isles. The Penny Black simplified the postal system. The postal system had actually been around for a couple of hundred years, but it was generally pretty awful and unreliable.

The old system was expensive, frustrating, and sometimes confusing (I covered the ancient postal system a little in my last book, 'A Romp with the Georgians', but I need to touch on it again here to give some background and to show how important the Penny Black really was).

You see, before the introduction of stamps, letters were charged by the number of pages they included. The envelopes themselves counted as a page of paper too, so you'd pay more in postage to put your letter inside an envelope. Envelopes then, were rarely used and so letters were folded over and sealed with wax. To get the most out of the old system, people wrote on the outside of a letter too, which saved them some money, by avoiding the cost of the envelope and the extra postage for sending it. The downside to this was the fact that anyone could read part of the letter's contents, if they got close enough. Servants, postmen, other family members, could all take a peep, unless the letter was written in a lover's code, which was sometimes necessary!

Another way of saving money, as well as doing away with an envelope, was to 'cross-write' This is where one set of writing is written on top of another at an angle, so you'd get two pages for the price of one. Reading a cross-written letter today is tricky to the modern eye. You need to be able to ignore the top set of writing and read the notes below first and then be able to switch to the top set! Sounds difficult, but you soon get used to it and was completely normal for people at the time, and it meant you could effectively half your postage cost.

Also, prior to the Penny Black, the cost of posting a letter varied wildly, not only by the number of pages it contained, but by the distance it needed to travel. On top of that, it was the recipient who paid to have the mail delivered, not the sender, so no delivery then could ever be guaranteed. If the recipient refused to pay to receive the post, then the letter was discarded, never to be read. Therefore no one knew whether or not their letters would ever actually be delivered or read. A nightmare scenario if the message was urgent, an invitation, of some importance, or of course, an invoice!

So, after 1840 and with the introduction of the Penny Black stamp, a stamp by the way, no different to the kind you use today, the sender, as we do, paid up front for the postage charge, meaning that all letters posted, were actually delivered… and that was whether the recipient wanted to receive it or not! There was also no variation in delivery cost. ten miles or two hundred miles, it didn't matter, the cost was simply the price of the stamp. The stamp was, just like today, bought singularly or in strips from a post office. If purchased in a strip, then you'd need to cut out each individual stamp… perforations were added to them a few years later.

The Penny Black, as the name suggests cost one penny back in 1840. A penny then, in today's terms is worth around fifty pence, so a letter was sent reliably anywhere within The British Isles in 1840, cheaper than the cost today!

This then, for the British postal system, was a game-changer. The seismic effect the Penny Black had on Britain and soon the rest of the world was equivalent to the introduction of mobile phones in the late 20th century. Pre the mobile phone, the world had telephones, just like the world had a postal system pre the Penny Black, but both the mobile and the first postage stamp changed life fundamentally and for the better for the people living at the time.

Both of these inventions, overnight, enabled better, faster and more reliable communication. Communication which improved business links and therefore investments and growth throughout the country rapidly. Families were also able to keep in touch more regularly and in emergencies, no matter where they were located with the use of the mobile phone and with the newly invented stamp.

Something else that changed the way we communicated was the introduction of 'Pillar Boxes'. These free-standing, red turrets with slits in to deposit letters, which would then be collected by postmen, started appearing in Britain in 1852. Twelve years after the introduction of the first stamp. The pillar boxes saved people the effort of going to a post office and of course mail could be put 'in the post' twenty-four hours a day. Soon after the first post boxes arrived in Britain, pillar boxes began appearing all around the empire too. In places like India, Australia, Malta, Sri Lanka, The Bahamas and Gibraltar (many are still there in regular use today). Britain also exported the pillar box design to other countries for use in their own postal service and in 1922, after Ireland gained independence from the empire, the Irish Free State was established and the red pillar boxes, which had been there for seventy years or so, under British control were kept in use for the newly formed Irish postal service... they simply painted them green!

Interestingly, it's often believed that Penny Black stamps, being known as a British cultural icon, as famous in fact as Britain's red phone boxes, being so old and important, bearing in mind they were the first stamps ever produced in the world, are worth small fortunes today. Well, unfortunately, they're not! As surprising as it may seem, even though they were only produced for about a year, over sixty-eight million Penny Black stamps were printed by the post office! The very best example in mint condition might be worth a few thousand pounds, but you've got more chance of winning the lottery than finding one of these. An average, but nevertheless fascinating bit of British and empire history, in the form of a Penny Black stamp can be bought for under £50.

The reason The Penny Black only lasted a year was due to its poor choice of colour. Each Penny Black, once it was licked and stuck onto an envelope and put into the postal system was then of course marked by the post office as used, just like today. The reason for this being obvious. To make sure that the stamp could not be peeled off and used again, without someone paying the penny postal charge.

The colour of the ink used to stamp the cancellation mark across the Penny Black was red and it was soon discovered that the red ink was often hard to see on the black background of the stamp. This meant that the less scrupulous users of the postal system were able to reuse many a Penny Black if the red ink wasn't visible on a used stamp. Each time, they'd beat the system and save a penny in doing so. And you won't be surprised to hear that a lot of people made a habit of reusing these stamps whenever they could! So, with all these Penny Blacks flying around the postal system for free, this began to cost the Royal Mail bags of money and equal irritation. A solution needed to be found and quickly. The solution was actually quite simple. Just reverse the colours around… the stamp became red, and the ink became black. Black ink on the red background of the stamp was obviously visible and the fraudulent reusing of the stamps pretty much came to an end. And this was the birth of the Penny Red stamp.

If you think it's impressive that the Royal Mail produced sixty-eight million Penny Blacks in a year, wait till you hear how many Penny Reds they printed. No one knows for sure the exact figure, but without doubt, over twenty-one billion Penny Reds went into active service, until they were replaced in 1879.

If you fancy starting a stamp collection, a Penny Red would be a great one to get it going. Not surprisingly, bearing in mind the numbers produced, you can buy one online very cheaply and from as little as a few pounds. They're remarkably pretty and really are lovely miniature pieces of art that look great mounted in a frame and hung on a wall. Something that might surprise you however is just how much money the rarer Penny Red stamp is worth!

The rarest of them all is the Penny Red plate 77. The plate 77 relates to the printing plate number for that edition of the stamps. Each printing plate was produced to create hundreds of thousands, if not millions of stamps, and each stamp that came off any particular plate carried the number of its plate on the outside edge of it. Nothing unusual at all, you'll find tiny numbers printed around the edge of all Penny Red stamps. But what make the plate 77 version of the Penny Red exceptionally rare is the fact that it should never have existed!

The printing plate number 77, you see, was faulty. A sample run of stamps was printed off it in 1863, but on inspection, officials at the post office were not satisfied with the quality of the printing. Under these circumstances, it was normal for the sample stamps to be destroyed, along with the printing plate, and another made in its place.

However, no one knows how, but a small number (it's thought, nine) of the plate 77 faulty Penny Red stamps made it out into circulation. No one knows who within the postal system released them either, it's a complete mystery. All we know, is that a few inferior quality Penny Reds from the printing plate 77, did see the light of day and were not destroyed as they should have been... and ever since the day that the defective plate 77s were inadvertently released, stamp hunters, collectors and investors the world over have lived and died searching for what has been described as the holy grail of philately and the most desirable and iconic of all British stamps... the faulty Penny Red, plate 77!

Rumour has it, that there are still a few undiscovered plate 77s out there, somewhere in the world, just waiting to be found... if you've got a Penny Red at home, you really need to examine it very carefully and with a magnifying glass. Look for the plate numbers around the outside edge. They'll be tiny and printed faintly within the pattern of the stamp. If you're lucky enough to see the two magical numbers together, the two 7s, then you might be in for a windfall of somewhere around half a million pounds... watch out though, there are fakes about!

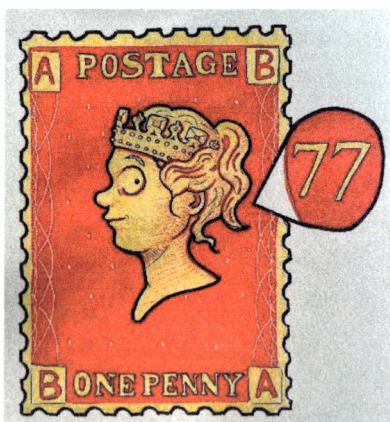

The Penny Red, plate 77… look for the almost hidden number 77!

And if you think half a million pounds is expensive for a stamp, there's another rarity that makes the plate 77 look like a cheap £50 Penny Black! It's an empire stamp too, and it's from the colony of British Guiana (now known as Guyana) in South America.

The stamp itself is known as the 'British Guiana 1c black on magenta' and it is an astonishingly rare and valuable stamp. In fact, it's the most valuable stamp in the world.

The story of this particular stamp and its creation is also astonishing. It dates to 1856 and was commissioned in British Guiana by the local postmaster there, an Englishman by the name Mr E.T.E Dalton. It was not normal for employees of the post office to issue their own stamps, but on this occasion, Mr Dalton had no other option. Living in an outpost of the empire, he'd been waiting for a shipment of stamps to be delivered to him. These stamps came by sea, but there was a delay in delivery due to some heavy storms in the Atlantic and he'd run out of stamps at the post office in British Guiana. Left with no alternative and in desperate need of stamps, Dalton commissioned local printers Joseph Baum and William Dallas to print an emergency issue for the post office. The printers were given the brief and the design for the stamps, but Baum and Dallas took it upon themselves to enhance the appearance of the stamp by adding their own depiction of a sailing ship to the centre of it. The postmaster wasn't exactly pleased by this, but nonetheless he needed the stamps and so the locally produced, temporary versions were put into circulation. Mr Dalton, as well as being slightly put out by the printer's taking it upon themselves to 'improve' his design, was also concerned that the new stamps might well be forged (or sneakily and secretly printed by Baum and Dallas), so to protect the post office from any possible shenanigans by locals attempting to get away with not paying for their post, or worse, profiteering by selling forged stamps, he instructed that all temporary stamps must be checked and signed off as genuine by a member of his staff within the local post office and before they were allowed into the postal system. They'd do this by physically inspecting the stamp and then signing it off as genuine with their initials across the stamp itself, if they were satisfied it wasn't a fake… the potential problems were solved, and the British Guiana post office was back in action… in true empire spirit!

Fast forward to the 21st century and one of the fabled British Guiana 1c black on magenta stamps, dated 1856 and believed to be the only one left in the world, came onto the market for sale. This one was obviously checked and signed off by one of Mr Dalton's postal clerks, a chap called E.D. Wight, as it carried his initials across it. The most sought-after stamp in the world sold in a New York auction, after a furious bidding war in 2014 for 9.5 million dollars!

Wherever the Empire governed, from Guiana in South America to Cape Town in South Africa, it set up a postal service based on its formula which was perfected back in Britain. The Indian postal service, as an example, was established in 1854 by the British and is the foundation of today's Indian post office.

As well as spreading around the world, the British postal system just kept getting better at home. By the 1890s, if you lived in London, you could expect twelve deliveries and collections of mail per day. Beginning at seven-thirty in the morning and finishing with the last post at seven-thirty in the evening. Birmingham received around six per day and even out in the countryside villages and towns, the postal system was more regular than it is today! It was so good in fact that friends, who lived miles away from one another could and did play chess together using the postal system. Two office workers, as an example, sitting in different locations across London could easily pass the time of day by playing chess by mail, whilst supposedly working in their respective places of employment! One opponent might start the game at seven-thirty in the morning, by posting his opening move on his way to work in one of the many pillar boxes. He'd receive the first counter move in the post by nine-thirty, whilst sat at his office desk (it would of course be disguised as work related mail). He'd be able to scan his opponents move and immediately reply with a counter-attack. The game could go on all day, or be carried over into the next, giving them both something to look forward to at work!

Invitations for dinner, offers to meet up for drinks, or replies to adverts in newspapers were all turned around in a matter of hours. Negotiations took place by mail. Back and forth, several times using the postal system, to buy a second-hand horse drawn carriage, sight unseen, was all normal stuff and the deal could be completed on the same day… just like negotiating for and buying a car on eBay!

None of this was out of the ordinary at the time and all of it was done remarkably efficiently using the Royal Mail postal service… Not quite as quick as email or text messaging, but just as effective!

Keeping on the subject of communication

The All Red Line

The 'Internet' of the day was something called 'The All Red Line' (I mentioned it above when talking about Bovril). This was a telegraph system that linked the British Empire around the globe. Called the 'All Red Line' simply because when you looked at the world map, showing the territories of the empire, they were all coloured red and the telegraph line, connecting countries to continents, across the high seas was shown on the map as a red line.

The project began in the 1850s with the laying of the first transatlantic cable line. Special cable ships strategically lowered thousands of miles of armoured telegraph lines onto the bottom of the ocean floor. At the same time, massive telegraph construction programmes were traversing vast areas of land across the world.

By 1872, telegraph messages could be sent from London, direct to Australia within minutes… sending a message by mail to Australia could take four months, so the telegraph link was space age technology at the time.

By 1870, the recently opened Suez Canal which connects the Mediterranean to the Indian Ocean, cut the travel time by ship from London to Bombay by twenty-three days and four thousand four hundred miles. This was an incredible time saver in travel terms, but also a huge money saver too. Trade with India and the rest of the empire back and forth grew hugely as goods became cheaper and more readily available for consumers all over the world. Britain took control of The Suez Canal in 1882, to protect her route through to India, from the effects of an Egyptian civil war. By this point Britain owned part of the canal anyway, after Egypt sold it to Britain to raise much needed cash. Having command of the canal to protect her trade, was vital for the empire's growth. This, along with the fast-developing all red line telegraph system, really opened up the whole of the near and far east to Britain and business boomed.

The cost of the telegraph laying programme, as you can imagine, was astonishingly high, but the benefits in the form of super-fast communication throughout the empire were even more astonishing. By 1911, the 'All Red Line' was finally complete and the empire was wired up for almost instantaneous communication. And the timing was fortuitous, because this meant that come the Great War, a few years later in 1914, Britain and her empire were able to communicate throughout the conflict uninterrupted and in real time. As hard as she tried, Germany was unable to cut the empire's communications to disrupt their war effort. This without doubt was a deciding factor in the outcome of the First World War.

One of the ships employed to work as a cable layer was the magnificent 'S.S. Great Eastern'. She, in her heyday was the largest ship ever built. Constructed from iron, she was launched in 1858 and was designed by one of the empire's great engineering giants, Isambard Kingdom Brunel. She carried four thousand passengers and was the first ship to be able to sail from England to Australia non-stop, without the need for refuelling. After her glory days as a passenger liner, she was converted for laying the 'All Red Line' telegraph cables, and after that she spent her final days moored up on the river Mersey in Liverpool as a party boat… a floating music hall!

When it came to empire engineers, Isambard Kingdom Brunel was up there with the best of them. However countless British engineering firms, with thousands of British workers around the country, designed, prefabricated, produced and assembled on site, some of the empire's most iconic structures and all over the empire too!

Here's just a few

The Victoria Falls Bridge. This is the bridge that not only connects the two countries of Zimbabwe and Zambia, but the one that has the most stunning view of Victoria Falls itself. The falls being one of the seven natural wonders of the world.

The idea of building the bridge at the time in 1902 was described by experts, as, 'A concept that was so bold, that it was to the point of arrogance' (something that was said a lot about people with big ideas during the British Empire)!

The experts continued to predict that building a bridge of this size and magnitude in the middle of what they then described as a deserted jungle was ridiculous… however, the empire builders were known for taking on ridiculous challenges. Challenges that no one else in their right minds would attempt!

The bridge was a small part of what was an attempt in the late 19th and early 20th century to build a railway line from

Cape Town in South Africa to Cairo in Egypt. This was not just any old working bridge though. It spanned over one hundred and fifty meters across the raging Zambezi River and at a dizzy height of one hundred and twenty-eight meters. It also needed to look good, which it did, and on top of that, instructions were given to engineers to 'build a bridge across the Zambezi where the trains, as they pass, will catch the spray of the Falls'.

The bridge was built in sections in the northeast of England by The Cleveland Bridge and Engineering Company, shipped to Africa and assembled on the banks of the Zambezi. It took fourteen months to build and was opened in 1905. The bridge is still there, still working as well today as it did then. It carries trains, cars and foot passengers between the two countries on a daily basis, and when the falls are in full flood, the bridge, as it was designed to do, is bathed in the spray from the Victoria Falls, or more correctly and in the local dialect: *Mosi-oa-Tunya*, meaning 'The Smoke That Thunders',

The railway line known as the 'Cape to Cairo', or the 'Red Line' (a term obviously borrowed from the telegraph cable laying project), was the dream and brain child of Cecil John Rhodes, one of Africa's biggest players at the time and a highly contentious figure, both then and today (because he is such a divisive character, I'll give a short history of his life in Africa a little later in the book).

The Cape to Cairo was designed, like the telegraph cables, to connect all English-speaking colonies, from the tip of Africa to the very top. This was of course for trade and expansion purposes, but also for vital protection in times of war and conflict. And just like in America, when they expanded their railway lines, it was expected that towns and cities would sprout up along the route, allowing commerce to flourish.

The audacious project was doomed to failure though due to the outbreak of, first of all, the Great War in 1914 which took much needed supplies, men, money and equipment away from the endeavour. A few years later, the Great Depression of the 1930s pressed the pause button for a while. Then came the Second World War, which just about bankrupted the empire and, after that, the decolonisation of Africa began, with the establishment of new independent countries, and brought the project to an end.

The Sydney Harbour Bridge

The famous Sydney Harbour Bridge was opened in 1932 and built by the company Dorman Long in Middlesbrough, England. The design of it was modelled on the Tyne Bridge in Newcastle, just up the road from the engineering works — a bridge Dorman Long built a few years prior. A classic empire shape and design that has stood the test of time, as both bridges are still in perfect working order and icons in their respective cities. Don't think for one moment though that empire designs were anything new or exclusive to British engineers. Empire builders had no problem copying styles, methods and techniques from others. Just as the painter Pablo Picasso said, 'Good artists copy, great artists steal'. British empire architects and engineers admired all sorts of creations around the world and in the nicest possible way, stole from them often! Both the Sydney Harbour Bridge and The Tyne Bridge are modelled on the earlier 'Hell Gate Bridge' built by the Americans in New York!

Hundreds of bridges built by the British Empire around the world, are still there, working as well today as they did when they were built. They have become the Roman roads of their time.

It wasn't just the rest of the world that benefited from the empire bridge builders either. Those back in Britain also got their fair share and a good example is the record breaking Forth Bridge opened in 1890. Constructed to carry rail traffic on the Edinburgh to Aberdeen line over the massive Forth of Firth estuary. Not only did it improve local travel, but the bridge also reduced the travel time from London to Aberdeen by train from thirteen hours to ten and a half hours.

For over twenty years, it was the longest single cantilever bridge in the world and just six weeks into the Second World War, the very first German air attack on Britain took place over the top of it. This was in October 1939 when twelve Junkers bombers attacked Navy ships nearby and were fought off by Supermarine Spitfire fighters… It became known as 'The Battle of the River Forth'.

The Forth Bridge, in recent years has been voted Scotland's greatest man-made wonder. A remarkable compliment to its designers and builders, bearing in mind, Scotland is not short of stunning man-made structures, in the form of castle, abbeys and monuments.

Ever since the massive bridge opened, a common saying appeared amongst English speaking people around the empire. A saying that was used when describing a job that looked like it might be never ending. So, when describing a house so large for example, someone might say that cleaning it would be like painting The Forth Bridge. In other words, as soon as you've finished the job, it would take so long, you'd need to start at the beginning again!

St Paul's Cathedral

There is more than one St Paul's Cathedral!

There's the one built by the British in Kolkata (previously Calcutta) India. This was completed in 1847 and built in the Indo-Gothic manner. It's a fusion of classic, traditional British style, complimented with ancient high Indian architecture. A design the British loved in India and one which gave a nod to the past rulers of the country, the Mughals in particular. It was a celebration of two distinctly different styles, which in architectural terms have stood the test of time well. The British built hundreds of buildings across India like this. From palaces for Indian regional rulers, libraries, town halls, Embassy's, the Parliament buildings in Delhi (inspired by an 11th Century Indian temple) and even shopping malls, 19th century style! The majority are still standing and in use today.

There is also a St Paul's Cathedral in Melbourne, Australia. Built in 1891.

Invention of Tin Cans… Some say, The British Empire was built on tin cans!

Yes, the humble tin can was instrumental in the expansion and success of the British Empire. On long and deep expeditions into unknown, uncharted and dangerous territories, stocks of tinned food, which were easy to transport, almost unbreakable and edible, either cooked, or uncooked, regularly meant the difference between a successful military campaign and defeat, arriving safely in a destination, or death in the wilderness. It also meant that new colonial settlements in the most isolated of locations could survive for much longer periods of time, without having regular food supplies delivered with great difficulty and expense, as would be expected. If the Brits didn't have hundreds of tins of salty corned beef and baked beans stashed in their stores, they'd have perished in no time!

The very first tin cans were invented in the early 19th century. The rush to find a reliable, cheap and safe food storage vessel began when the French emperor, Napoleon Bonaparte ran a competition amongst French inventors. This was during the Napoleonic wars with Britain. He challenged his scientists to find a method of preserving food for long periods of time. Fighting the British was taking place all over Europe and North America, so troops and supplies needed to be moved huge distances and for very long periods of time. Napoleon was also planning an invasion of England with three hundred thousand troops (which were ready to go) and they, he knew, needed a good supply of French produced food, otherwise, it was thought, the British cuisine might kill them off!

The French were mainly developing glass jars for the purpose, but the British, obviously inspired by the French, were the first to develop the game-changing tin can for the job.

It was Englishman Peter Durand who got the credit and he patented the idea of a tin can in 1810. After some experimental voyages, sending his canned food on trips around the world with the Royal Navy, which were mightily successful, he, rather than going into production himself, sold the concept and the patent to another pair of Englishmen, Bryan Donkin and John Hall. Durand received one thousand pounds for his invention, the equivalent of around eighty thousand pounds today. Durand went on to patent and sell the idea in America too.

Soon after, in 1813 the world's first commercial canning factory was set up by Donkin & Hall in London and they began supplying food for the Royal Navy. Later, they canned fuel, gunpowder, and even agricultural seeds. These seeds were transported safely for months, across the empire to introduce new and much needed food crops to regions where not enough indigenous food, grew naturally.

It's fair to say that the tin can invention was instrumental to the success of the British Empire. With tinned food lasting for not just weeks and months, but for years on end, the stuff was able to sustain the greatest power the world had ever known in history for very long periods of time. Therefore, its pioneers, wherever they travelled across the globe, wherever they settled, they had a ready food supply, which could maintain them long enough to build outposts, trading centres or permanent settlements. The tin can, also gave them time to develop or grow other local food sources. The British had a lot to thank the tin can for!

Another great invention, which is kind of related to the tin can was the Thermos Flask. This was invented by Englishman James Dewar in 1872. Dewar came up with a vacuum jacketed goblet, designed to keep liquids warm (ideal for Bovril!) and twenty years later, a similar design, especially to keep liquids cool (ideal for trekking across some tropical wilderness) was exhibited in 1892.

Unfortunately for Dewar, he never patented his invention of the flask, which was up until this point known as the 'Dewar Flask'. This was a terrible mistake on his behalf, because in 1904, two German industrialists took out a patent on the design and called it after their company, 'Thermos'. And so, they patented the 'Thermos Flask'!

Dewar sued Thermos, but lost the case, and his design, frustratingly for him to say the least, was forever known as the Thermos Flask. Although, scientists around the world often refer to it as the 'Dewar Flask' in recognition of its inventor.

Sport

The Indian originals of Snooker

You can thank the British Empire for the invention of Snooker!

Army officers stationed in India during the period of the British Raj often had very little to do, so they needed plenty of sports and pastimes to occupy their time and entertain themselves, day and night.

First of all, here's a bit of background information to get a feel for the time and the place, which created the perfect environment for the invention of snooker!

Officially, Britain took control of India and brought her into her empire in 1858 — although Britons, working for The East India Company had been there, in positions of power, for a couple of hundred years and in almost complete control since the 1750s. The East India was a huge trading company, given a royal charter by Queen Elizabeth I in 1600 to go out into the world, explore, colonise and trade. Other European monarchs were issuing charters to their own explorers and merchants to do exactly the same and it was a race between the European nations to find and cultivate the most profitable markets.

The East India Company was remarkably successful.

So successful and powerful in fact that they even had their own standing army of two hundred thousand men. Twice the size of the British army! They also had a company flag, just like a country would have. A flag under which, its soldiers, who were mainly Indian, but with British officers, literally fought and died in wars over money, trade and land. To give them credit where it's due, they were also pretty good at keeping the peace between warring neighbours... but only when it suited them!

The East India Company flag

You could never describe the company's business practises as being exactly ethical, especially if viewed from a distance of a few hundred years in the future but supplying opium (an illegal and highly addictive drug) to Chinese merchants in return for tea, as an example, was perfectly normal at the time! The fact that opium then killed many thousands of addicts in China was not much of a concern to the directors of the company, or the Chinese distributors in China, all of whom were making eye watering sums of cash out of the drugs deal... not much really changes!

So much cash was being generated in fact, that the East India Company effectively became a world power in itself! Helped and supported by the British Government, who of course benefited through taxation and trade deals.

Things changed dramatically for the company though in the mid-1800s. They pushed their luck too far with increasingly heavy taxation on the locals and constant wars with Indian internal states, who decided not to toe the company line. The East India Company, through its mistakes and miscalculations was responsible for causing the infamous and bloody Indian Mutiny of 1857. This was the beginning of the end for the company.

Ill feelings had been building for a very long time amongst the company's troops, known as 'Sepoys'. These were the private soldiers who made up the vast majority of The East India's massive army. There were tens of thousands of Sepoys in the employ of the company and they, en mass, along with hundreds of thousands of fellow Indians from all parts of the vast territory rebelled against the 'Company' rule in India... and so started a vicious war, full of terrible retribution on both sides.

Prior to the mutiny, and for a good hundred years, the East India Company had been able to make profitable agreements, based on business deals and alliances with hundreds of the states and over two thousand tribes that made up the subcontinent of India. Indian nationalism is a modern phenomenon. During the 18th and 19th centuries, most people did not associate themselves with being Indian. The vast majority only held allegiances with their tribe, clan, ethnic group or religion. Had the area been unified as a country, it would have been impossible for the British to have any influence there.

Because of the deals made with the British, the individual rulers of the hundreds of states, governing over millions of subgroups of people, grew very rich indeed. Along, of course with the East India Company directors, its merchants, suppliers and hangers-on. And because this vast area of land, that was around fifteen times the size of Britain, was not unified and the individual states constantly at war with one another, it was ripe picking and easy enough for the East India to work closely with the multitude of ruling princes and Maharajahs that supported the company's goals... the main goal, which suited them beautifully, was to make stacks of cash!

With so many indigenous rulers onside, the company was able to literally fight off those states that were against it and its local allies. It was a system that worked efficiently enough. That is of course until the Indian Mutiny of 1857.

The mutiny, or rebellion as it's also called had many causes and the tensions had been building for many years. Political, social, financial, and religious in nature, but it was the introduction in 1857 of the new gunpowder cartridges for the Enfield rifle that sparked the mayhem and bloodletting. The Enfield was the rifle of choice used by the East Indian Company and its Indian Sepoys. To load the rifle, a soldier needed to tear open the greased cartridge with his teeth, but the new cartridge was rumoured, for water proofing reasons, to be covered in cow, or pig fat, which meant on religious grounds, the soldiers refused to even handle the cartridges. With cows being sacred to Hindus and pigs being unclean and untouchable to Muslims, the very idea of putting these cartridges in the soldiers' mouths was abhorrent, against their religion and something they point blank refused to do.

The arrogance of the company directors must be acknowledged here. They knew well enough that the animal fat covered cartridges would be offensive to its multiple thousands of troops, but profit and efficient weapons were much more important than the sensibilities of its soldiers! A seriously bad mistake, which cost them dearly. The cartridge issue ignited old grievances and pretty well immediately, whole army units of Sepoys deserted the army and joined forces with peasant groups and mini armies funded by noncompliant Indian princes, who were always opposed to The East India Company anyway and saw this as an opportunity to destroy them and their Indian ally's.

The mutiny lasted eighteen months and was vicious beyond believe, with almost unparalleled hatred and ferocity. Massacres and cruelties were inflicted by both sides and retribution punishments were particularly barbaric.

The British adopted a favourite execution practise from the old Mughal empire rulers called 'Blowing', This is where the condemned prisoner is tied with his back to the mouth of a cannon, before the gun is fired. The result was of course, obliteration. The victims head would shoot high into the air, with some accounts saying as high as fifty feet. The arms in turn, flew off right and left for a hundred feet or more and the legs slumped to the ground. The body parts would be left to be picked over by vultures. This was not just a horrible way to die, but it sent a message to would be rebels to keep in line.

And to add insult, they also on occasions forced Muslim mutineers to chew pork before being hung. Hindus might be smothered in cow fat. Again, this was to send reverberations of fear and horror through the population, in the hope that it would stop them rebelling!

The rebels themselves were just as cruel. Mass murder and rapes were commonplace and they'd execute and torture prisoners in public, again to send a message. This time to any Indians who were thinking of supporting the British.

And as public executions go, there was one that when reported in the British press, filled readers with horror.

The massacre of Satichaura Ghat in 1857 was where many hundreds of British troops and civilians, who were under siege from rebel fire in the town of Cawnpore, were tricked into leaving the relative safety of the town's walls. Cawnpore was an important British garrison town, strategically located on The Trunk Road, that famous trade route across India. But after a long and arduous siege, a ceasefire was reached and the surviving British, it was agreed, would be given a supposed safe passage by the mutineers. They were, it was agreed and arranged, that the men, women and children would be allowed to trek to the river Ganges and board several boats moored nearby at the river landing known as Satichaura Ghat and thence sail down the river to safety.

But, just as the British had nearly finished boarding the vessels, the boatmen, who they thought were about to sail them to safety, set fire to the thatched roofs of the boats, jumped overboard and began swimming to the riverbanks. This, it seems was the signal to the waiting rebels, hiding on both sides of the river to open fire on the British. Some of the British were armed and shot back, but they were completely outnumbered. A couple of boats did manage to slip away and they drifted downstream, to be followed by the rebels and most were captured and killed. But, once the firing stopped on the moored boats, the rebel foot soldiers went in, armed with swords, pistols, battle axes and spears to finish off some more and to take prisoners. The prisoners, it was planned, would be used as hostages, bargaining chips and human shields against an expected British retaliation.

These killings were a planned attack, and this was an organised execution. Some accounts say that local villagers, who were made aware of the upcoming event, travelled from miles around to witness it. It's estimated that several thousands of people came to watch the execution.

Some of the British soldiers taken hostage that day, were later executed, but around two hundred women and children were kept as prisoners in Cawnpore, the town of course, the rebels had just captured. However, sometime later, British forces, after some fighting, retook the town. They immediately went searching for the hostages, who they assumed had been left behind by the retreating rebels. What they discovered however was a massacre of unbelievable proportions. Every one of the two hundred or so women and children had been shot or stabbed to death and their bodies thrown into the town's only well and water supply.

The reaction from the British once the massacre had been fully discovered was one of rage and retribution. The British garrison went on a surge of violence against any in the local population who couldn't prove that they had nothing to do with the massacre of the women and children. In truth, this was impossible to prove, so many were killed on the spot, hung, 'blown' from cannons, or shot.

From then on and throughout the rest of the mutiny, the British war cry to fire the troops up for battle was 'Remember Cawnpore'.

Neither side in this conflict conducted themselves honourably, but this idea of behaving so called honourably in war, is mainly a made-up concept for Hollywood movies. The British, out of all nations, gained a reputation for playing by the rules when it came to war, but war, by its very nature, can be dirty and this was a perfect example of that. One dastardly deed from one side, spawned something equal or worse from the other and so it went on.

It is estimated that there were forty thousand Europeans living in India at the time and around six thousand were killed (one in seven) as opposed to around eight hundred thousand Indians who died. This number was made up of both those on the rebel side and those fighting for the British.

The British and The East India Company were victorious in the end. They defeated the rebels and the uprising was put down. But this would not have been possible without the loyalty of the majority of the Indian troops, especially the highly regarded warriors, the Sikhs. And even though many rebelled, the majority of the princes and Maharajahs, with their signed lucrative trade treaties, also supported the British, for obvious financial reasons. Without them, the British would have been banished.

Even though the war was won, it spelt the end of the East India Company's rule in India. In the aftermath of the bloody uprising, which could and should have been foreseen and halted by the East India company, the British government effectively abolished the company in 1858. The Crown itself now took over all of its possessions, its army, administration and its taxing powers. Now the British government ruled India and along with assistance from the continent's princes and Maharajahs, the period known as the British Raj was born. It lasted eighty-nine years, coming to an end with Indian Independence in 1947, just after the Second World War.

In India's history, empires have come and gone many times over, and over countless generations (at least ten major empires have ruled there in the past two thousand years or so) but the British Empire was the last one to occupy that huge land mass of the Indian subcontinent… and we can thank all of the above for the invention of Snooker!

So, back to the officer's mess during the period of the British Raj in 1875. The men were always looking for new ways to entertain themselves of an evening. They'd been playing billiards for some time, but one officer, a lieutenant Neville Francis Fitzgerald Chamberlain, whilst playing around with some new ideas on the billiard table, decided to introduce some extra, coloured balls, just to spice things up a bit. No one quite knew what they were doing, but over time, with experimentation, they developed a new form of the billiard game, allocating points scored for different colours, order of potting, etc. The game though had no name and not many people really understood what the new rules were, especially as they were developing, so anyone playing this new form of billiards for the first time was referred to as a 'snooker'. A snooker was the slang term for a new raw recruit at the Royal Military Academy in Woolwich, back home in old Blighty. Chamberlain observed that everyone playing his new game were raw recruits to it and therefore, they were called 'snookers'… in no time the name stuck, and the game of snooker was born.

The Maharajahs loved the game too and it eventually became popular back in Britain. The popularity is credited to the then Billiard's champion, John Roberts, who, when visiting India from England went to meet Chamberlain for dinner at one of his Maharajahs friend's palaces. Here, they discussed the rules and sequence of events of the new game 'snooker'.

Roberts returned home to England and introduced snooker to the British, where the popularity of it grew over time. In 1916, the first official snooker competition in the world took place in England and the first professional event was staged in 1927. By the 1930s, snooker had become more popular than billiards in Britain and it was the most popular and played cue sport right across the empire.

Let's keep on the subject for a while of sports invented during the British Empire.

We'll start with football and rugby. Both sports you can thank the time of the British Empire for. A game that resembled football had been played for centuries, but there were no rules to it whatsoever. Matches often went on for hours without a break and some even lasted several days. Leather footballs hadn't been invented, so blown up pig's bladders were the ball of choice! Any number of players were able to take part and believe it or not, during the 18th century, one game in Derby had over one thousand players! Pitches could be any size too and when competing villages played one another, each village had their own set of goal posts… therefore, the posts could easily be several miles away from one another! Kicking other players in the shins was perfectly acceptable. This was called 'shinning' and a player could 'shin' anyone he liked, including a member of his own team! Drunkenness was often a problem at an organised game of football too. Not dissimilar to more modern football matches, where rowdy crowds drink too much alcohol before entering the ground. The difference being though, with the old football matches, that the drunkenness was more likely to be on the pitch, than amongst the spectators!

But it was the more organised game of football that developed in England during the second half of the 19th century that spread across the world and eventually became the most popular sport played anywhere in the empire. From Africa to Australia.

It was two prominent schools that first played something like the modern game of football. These were Rugby and Eton. At Rugby the rules included the ability to pick up the ball with the hands and this developed into the game we know today, named after the school, called 'rugby' and it became referred to as 'the running game'.

At Eton on the other hand, they had different rules to their version of the field ball sport. Their rules dictated that no player could pick up the ball, as this for them, was a game played exclusively with the feet. It was referred to as 'the dribbling game'.

The two types of game were played not just by these exclusive fee-paying schools either, but elsewhere too. The sports' popularity increased, especially amongst the working classes, for whom the games were easy and cheap to organise and needed nothing but a ball and a field. But deciding on firm and proper rules for both games proved difficult to agree and no one school, or organisation, had the authority to actually set those rules. Therefore, both games were only played by amateur enthusiasts and the games were played by varying rules, in different parts of the country.

But, eventually, in 1863 the first football association was established in London. There, they agreed that the two games would be finally separated. Football would be just that. A game played with the feet (and head) with no hands allowed and the Rugby school version would have its own rules, where the ball could indeed be picked up and ran with. Ball size and weight were agreed, player numbers, timings, pitch sizes and general rules of the sports were written down, signed off and adhered too. It was now that the two games officially separated into 'association football' and 'rugby'. And from then on, both sports flourished and quickly spread across the world.

When it came to the empire, sport like football, rugby and of course cricket were seen as excellent ways to prepare young men in the public schools of Britain to go out into the world and expand the empire. These sports developed not just fitness and strength, but also taught teamwork, solidarity, self-control, initiative, a little bit of adventurous risk taking, a sense of belonging and a duty to one's teammates. These are all qualities required to maintain and build the largest empire the world had ever seen. Sport then, was as important as academic studies and in some cases even more valuable. Young men, when applying for a position in the imperial services to work abroad somewhere within the massive empire machinery, would be required to take an academic test of sorts. However, in many cases, more attention was paid to an applicant's athletic record as a sportsman from their school days, than their academic abilities… such was the importance of recognised team players for the good of the empire.

Cricket

Cricket, invented in the south of England, became the country's national sport during the 18th century. It was also the perfect game to export throughout the empire and to every colony.

Living abroad, often in tropical conditions, quite alien to the average Briton, the playing of tradition home grown team sports helped keep the bonds strong between the colonials. Cricket was the ideal game for this. It could be played even in intense heat and it was thought of as the most important game anyone could and should play throughout the empire… and for the good of the empire. Cricket matches allowed different sections of colonial society to come together in a bonding exercise. It kept community cohesion strong amongst the 'Brits abroad' and was often the social highlight of the week, where whole families could spend the day mixing and relaxing in good and alike company. This was seen as being good for mind and soul. It helped keep the British, British, no matter where in the world they found themselves.

Tennis also transferred well across the empire, particularly with the wealthier colonialists who often built tennis courts in their gardens, not necessarily to play on, but more importantly to show off to their neighbours!

Six of the world's ten most popular sports were invented by the British. So, you can add table tennis, hockey and golf to the list above. Even American Football and Baseball have their roots firmly planted in Britain.

Sport unifies nations, brings people of different cultures together and unites in a way nothing else can. Countries around the Empire were able to communicate and interact with one another through the medium of sport. Sport was a 'getting to know you' exercise. It helped build relationships and business connections and was part of the glue that kept the empire together.

Union Jack or Union Flag?
So, the British used sport to prepare young men to go out into the world and spread what they believed were the greatest values in the world (British ones) in an attempt to civilise the globe and bring it all under one flag for peace and prosperity… that flag being, of course, The Union Jack.

And for those of you muttering to yourselves that the term I should use here when referring to the British flag, is simply the 'Union Flag' and that the term 'Union Jack' should only be used when the British flag is flown from a warship or other sea going vessel… you're wrong to mutter!

In 1908 the UK Parliament approved the verdict that 'The Union Jack' should be regarded as the 'National Flag'… so, the term is not just for boats, although the name probably has its origins at sea and dates back to the 17th century when Charles II proclaimed that the Union Flag should be flown by ships of the Royal Navy as a jack. A jack being a small flag. There you have it then. 'Union Flag' or 'Union Jack', they both mean the same thing and you can call the flag either name, wherever you're flying them!

Sport also played a huge role in not only keeping the British colonials occupied and entertained whilst in the tropics, but it was employed to build relationships with the local elites too. These were the natural leaders in their communities, whom the British needed on their side to be able to govern huge areas of land and incomprehensibly large populations.

To give you an idea of the populations involved. In India during the period of the Raj, merely one thousand British civil servants governed the day-to-day existence of over two hundred and eighty million people! This could never have happened without the consent of the population and that consent was gained through the relationships the empire built with the Indian nobility and the powerful. From the Maharajahs and princes to the village leaders in rural locations, many of whom, would never expect to ever meet in the flesh, in their lifetime, anyone from Britain. Millions of Indians filled the ranks of the British Indian army, the civil service, and the police. And one of the bonds that kept the whole bureaucratic and civil machine together... was sport.

With its strict code of conduct, unbendable rules and expected gentlemanly behaviour, cricket, especially, came to be seen as a great way of transmitting British imperial values across the world. The church was very much in favour of cricket too. One of the bishops' jobs was to send missionaries around the world, with the sole intent of converting the peoples of it, to Christianity. This would, as a by-product of being converted, also spread not only Christian beliefs, but just as importantly, spread civilisation too. Religion and civilisation went hand in hand. Cricket, they thought would be a handy game to teach a little bit of civilisation!

But, the great irony of the British transporting their sports around the world, is that many of the colonies' local inhabitants did indeed soon adopt the sports as their own. And soon played them better than the British!

India, famously took to cricket, especially amongst the high caste in society. One very well know Indian cricketer at the time was the future Maharajah of Nawanagar. Sir Ranjitsinhji Vibhaji Jadeja. Known as Ranji, he was educated in India and at Cambridge and he became famous throughout the empire as one of the most remarkable cricketers the game had ever produced. Even today, he's regarded as one of the best batsmen of all time. His technique was described as unorthodox and the most original in any player up to that point. He invented new types of defence and attack, which had the public and the newspapers in awe. One cricket commentator described him as "the midsummer night's dream of cricket", and another said "before the arrival of Ranji, cricket was English through and through, but when Ranji batted, a strange light from the East flickered in the English sunshine".

Ranji played for Cambridge University, Sussex (Captain) and England between 1895 and 1904. He brought an extra spark and adventure to the game and in doing so, inspired millions to pick up the bat and the ball. Cricket was never to be the same!

In the colonies, local teams, whether it be cricket or football took great pleasure in beating the British at their own game too. Many Indian teams even insisted on playing football in their bare feet against the Raj players. This was partly psychological on their behalf, as it really upset the British players, who were deeply concerned with the consequences of being beaten by a rag tag team of bare footed locals. The Brits turning up, kitted out with all the right gear, including technologically advanced, studded, laced up leather football boots, only to get thrashed by the bare footed locals, who couldn't stop knocking the heavy leather football, dozens of times past the British goal... much to the pleasure of the local crowds!

Even today, there is great and mostly friendly sporting rivalry between England and its many past colonies... ironically, this rivalry keeps the connections between the nations alive and well, so sport is still doing its job of bonding people together. Amusingly, it's the Australians, those people that mainly came from British stock, that take the greatest pleasure in giving England a good thrashing!

Language

As well as sport, the empire spread the English written and spoken language around the world. There is of course, the argument that English was forced upon people who would never have needed to speak it, but that aside, no one can deny that the British empire left a legacy of easy communication amongst people who under different circumstances would find it hard to, not only communicate, but to trade and build meaningful and even peaceful relationships with neighbours and other nations.

English today is spoken in one hundred and six countries, it's the accepted language of the internet, over ninety percent of airlines use it and the vast majority of music the world listens too is sung in English. The television we watch is mainly in English and even the majority of the scientific papers produced around the globe are printed in English. All of which is good for world trade, improvements in standards of living and of health and peace. You can thank the empire for that!

Christmas Crackers... if you're stuck for an interesting conversation over Christmas lunch, this will make you positively riveting!

Tom Smith was a London sweet maker and shop owner. During a trip to Paris for a holiday, he was naturally drawn to other sweet shops, and here he discovered the French were wrapping some of their Bon Bon's in pretty paper, adding interest and value for their clientele, which the French seemed to love. So, on his return, he copied what he'd seen and tried something similar in his own shop. However, the differences between the British consumer and the French were immediately obvious. His London clientele just couldn't get with the idea of having to remove paper from a sweet before eating it. This, to them was a waste of time and an added expense they didn't appreciate. They much preferred, simply sticking their hands in a paper bag and pulling out several sweets in one go! The idea then didn't take off and Tom quickly stopped wrapping his sweets in paper. Britain just wasn't ready for that sort of continental behaviour!

Although, the sweet wrapping experiment was unsuccessful, the experience of it planted a seed of an idea in Toms' head and one night, sat in front of his log fire at home, mesmerised by the flames and deep in thought. With no one else around, his living room was completely silent — apart from, that is, the noise coming from the direction of the fire. He was struck by the constant spitting, sparking and crackling coming out of the hearth and he couldn't help himself... he began concentrating on it.

This was the moment he was struck from nowhere, with a fabulous business idea! Never mind just sweets, how about, he thought, creating a novelty, surprise gift too, wrapped in card and paper, that when pulled open, would make a crackling noise, and even spark just like his fire was doing. Never knowing what was inside the gift box, would make quite a curiosity. Even his London clients would go for that!

Tom, immediately set to work experimenting with different wraps and boxes for his sweets and gifts. He met with a local fireworks company, who helped him design and build in the crackles, bangs, and sparks and eventually, after much trial and error, in 1861 Tom Smith launched his new range of novelty packages, containing delicious sweets and unusual surprise gifts which he called 'Bangs of Expectation' from his London sweet shop.

Soon, his invention became known simply as 'Crackers' and the business of making and selling them went from strength to strength.

When Tom died, the business was taken over by his three sons, who were just as passionate about their crackers as he was, and the brothers developed some new ranges (they were the ones who added paper hats to crackers). They travelled the world in search of new novelties and began adding more unexpected type gifts to their crackers. You know the kind of thing... gifts no one knew they needed! They also created unusual crackers for the more niche markets. So, special crackers were made for young single people, out and about on the dating scene. These contained humorous objects like funny false teeth, terrible chat up lines and imitation wedding rings. There were the more serious crackers too, for those interested in politics, for military personal, coronation specials and even for supporters of the new 'vote for women' campaign championed by the very interesting group known as the Suffragettes. (I'm coming to them soon!)

The ultimate crackers though were the ones known as the 'Millionaires'. These, as you can imagine were highly costly and contained solid silver boxes, which, when opened surprised a lucky person with a jewelled gift, or a small bar of gold!

Jokes soon started appearing in crackers and these were as bad then, as they are today!

Democracy

Britain's democracy at home was hard won. At the beginning of the British Empire, less than five percent of the population had the vote. Of that five percent, all were men, and all were independently wealthy enough to own property and land. In fact, that was the criteria. Only rich male property owners could vote in local or national elections, and these naturally were mainly from the aristocracy. This, as you can imagine didn't benefit very much the ninety-five percent of the population who were not rich and who didn't own property. They had no say in law making, or taxation, or in fact anything whatsoever that effected their lives. The elite minority ruled the majority and what they said, went.

However, steadily, as the empire grew, it also adapted the way it governed itself, making the system fairer to the growing population. With its power and wealth, the empire could have taken the route of dictatorship, ruling its subjects with an iron fist and continued distributing its wealth amongst a tiny percentage of effective oligarchs. Fortunately, it didn't take that route. The British Government eventually began to bow to pressure, especially from the expanding middle classes. These were the merchants, factory owners, the new shop keepers (and cracker manufacturers!), railway builders and entrepreneurs of the day. They were making a great deal of money for the country, and they wanted a say in its political and domestic life. The middle classes demanded a say in how the country was run, how much tax they'd be charged and where their tax money was going to be spent. The working classes too, who were toiling away in the new factories, in the coal mines and on the railways were highly vocal and also demanded their rights. They knew that without them, quite literally, the machinery of the empire, and therefore the workshop of the world, would grind to a halt.

In truth, talk, requests, and demands alone may not have been listened too. The British public were not averse to a bit of rioting to gain their rights and these riots, some of which were very violent, were increasingly troublesome for the government and the unrest certainly nudged them in the right direction. Huge strikes by the working classes began to take place. If the middle classes held some power, due to their money-making abilities (and therefore tax revenues) then the working classes held some power by threatening to withhold their labours. Strikes, riots and withholding of labour were not in the interests of commerce and the government knew that. When you're running an empire and Britain is supplying the world with everything from luxury high end goods to millions of tons of iron nails, the last thing you need are stoppages in factory production.

The Government reacted and so, from 1832, a number of acts began to be passed through Parliament, giving more people the vote. By 1867, thirty-two percent of Britain's population were eligible to vote and by 1884 it was around two-thirds of the population. A great improvement, but when one third of the population has no say in how their country is governed, it could never be described as a democratic state — especially when the majority of that one third without a vote, were women… and women were now, well and truly on the march!

Enter the Suffragettes!

Most people have a pretty good idea who and what the Suffragettes stood for, but I must talk about them here, as they were very much a product of the British Empire, and their success gave confidence to other women around the world. The confidence to call for their own vote. They're also, even today, role models for women in many other countries, who still, even now, do not enjoy their full political and human rights.

They accelerated the changes needed in Britain for a fully inclusive, one man (or woman), one vote, system. Without these women, the democracy we take for granted and the one that was exported around the world, would have taken a lot longer to arrive!

Here's some background information on this very special group of women. Some of it you'll know, but I'm quite sure, some of it, you won't!

The infamous 'Suffragettes' appeared in the very early years of the 20th century, and they were quite easy to spot with their brightly coloured sashes and were often seen riding bicycles. Suffragettes embraced bicycles. They were described as vehicles for 'fresh air and freedom' which pretty well summed up what the movement was looking to achieve for women!

The demand for change within the voting system, to allow women the vote had been going on for decades and the first major group of female campaigners began to make an impact on social and political life in the 1860s. This was when hundreds of women organised a petition to demand equal political rights for women. Thousands of signatures were gathered and handed in to parliament. The women had support from several high-profile male MP's too, but when the subject was debated in parliament, the suggestion was defeated. From then on, more and more female organisations formed to petition and pressure the government to make the changes which would include the vote for women. These women now became known as 'Suffragists'… but don't confuse this group of activists with the 'Suffragettes'. Although they both had the same aims and goals, their methods of achieving their right to vote, could not be further apart!

Suffragists adopted a non-confrontational approach to their demands. They were completely peaceful and believed that their argument was strong and moral enough for the message to get through to parliament. They had public support too from the majority and they naturally assumed that in no time, they'd be stood in line with the men on polling days.

Membership grew to around fifty-four thousand women, so this was no fringe movement. They held very organised public meetings (always peaceful), they produced posters, calendars, and signed petition after petition. All of this was done quite properly and legally. Their movement was listened too, tolerated and placated, but their demands and efforts, sadly, were to absolutely no avail!

In the early days, most of the Suffragists came from the middle, or upper classes and their calls for the vote for women, only really applied to those that were relatively wealthy and property owners… in other words, themselves! Things started to heat up a little when working class women began joining the organisations and calling themselves 'Suffragists'.

All women now, it seemed, wanted the vote and from all sections of the social class system. Even more pressure was piled onto parliament, but still, no one really listened and nothing changed.

However, frustrated with the lack of progress of the Suffragists, a more militant group of women burst onto the scene. They accused the Suffragists of being far too benign and soft in their approach. This, they said was proven by the fact that their campaigning had achieved little, or nothing. Their respectable, peaceful and legal methods were simply being sneered at by those in positions of power within parliament and so, it was believed, a new belligerent, militant approach was necessary!

Welcome the 'Suffragettes'. They were not a bit like the

'Suffragists'. They were militant in their nature and their motto summed them up perfectly… 'Deeds Not Words'!

In 1903, The Women's Social and Political Union was founded in Manchester by Emmeline Pankhurst, along with her daughters Christabel and Sylvia. The women only movement spread quickly around Britain and involved very many more working-class members than the groups that had gone before, so their social make-up was far more inclusive. This movement had an altogether new vibe and their attitude to campaigning was very different too. Never mind peaceful petitions, discussion groups and tea parties to raise funds and awareness. This lot were going to make themselves known to everyone in the country and very quickly indeed. They were taking what they called 'direct action', and this didn't involve pointless, polite requests either… they were all about 'shock and awe' and blimey, they didn't half shock the British establishment!

Soon then, newspapers had images of women covered in emblems and signs, carrying banners and flags, wrestling with big burly policemen, while getting arrested on the streets of Britain… this was radical stuff! They were also pictured chained to railings, gates and the doors of buildings. Journalists wrote articles about some of these women bursting into public meetings and causing terrible upset, disrupting the proceedings, knocking tables and chairs over and being rude and even violent to anyone who dared stand up to them! 'Votes for Women' was the chant, being shouted and screamed in all sorts of places around the country. The theatre, private parties, political meetings, on the streets and even outside of parliament… this, the seat of power of the biggest empire ever seen on earth. A group of Suffragettes, hundreds of them, en mass, even tried to storm the House of Commons, but the police were waiting for them and after a violent struggle, the invasion was thwarted. Violence was a tool much employed, and it was never taken off the cards. It was shouted loudly in the streets that the vote for women would be gained through 'any means necessary' and this was a worry for the government.

Even though, it was all about shock and awe, the marketing department at Suffragette headquarters even came up with a silent campaign to help spread the message of universal suffrage. This was a way of getting to even the most secluded parts of the country and to those members of the public, who didn't buy newspapers, or took much interest in social affairs. Everybody of course used coins. They had to, there was no other way of buying their daily supplies. With this in mind, the Suffragettes started mutilating Penny coins… they began stamping with hammer and branding tools, the words 'Votes For Women' right across the head of the monarch on thousands of the bronze coins. These small denomination coins then spread quickly around the country — each one carrying the message, which would be passed on and seen thousands of times each. With the pennies being of low value, they were banked infrequently and so the banks had little opportunity to remove them from circulation. Therefore, the coins just kept doing the rounds and silently promoting the campaign. This was very clever marketing. Completely illegal of course, but nevertheless, highly effective!

But back to being noisy. Window smashing was a popular Suffragette way of sending a message. If you were an MP, or a non-supporter, your windows were fair game! Others though moved on, to much more serious forms of vandalism. Setting fire to pillar boxes to upset the highly efficient Royal Mail service was a good way for them to attract attention, as was damaging public buildings and even burning them down. Prison sentences naturally followed, as Suffragettes poured through the court system. Prison though for the more hardcore members of the group, was a badge of honour, and if one crime didn't get them imprisoned, then, they'd soon commit another to make sure they were indeed eventually locked up at his majesty's pleasure. This was the aim... they wanted to be put in jail! And if the authorities thought that locking these troublesome women up in cells was a way of keeping them quiet for a while and stopping them from gaining any publicity, they were very much mistaken.

The Suffragettes discovered a new way of keeping their cause in the public's minds, even whilst in prison and to be mercenary about it, it was pure 'gorilla marketing' gold. This was the dangerous Suffragette hunger strike. Nothing quite like it had gone on before and the public were horrified and mesmerised at the same time. Stories of hunger striking women, lying out on metal beds, starving to death in barred cells, were being told and hugely exaggerated in pubs up and down the country. Naturally, newspaper sales shot up, much to the delight of the paper's owners, who kept the stories and illustrations coming in on a daily basis.

The hunger strike tactic proved to be a huge attention grabber and so as far as getting the Suffragettes message out there was concerned, it was a winner, although many women suffered terrible health consequences. This though was in the mind of the woman involved, a war and one that was worth at least suffering for and possibly even dying in aid of. The more militant women actually referred to themselves as soldiers, so it came as no surprise that some of them would go to such extremes in their fight for the simple right to vote.

Oddly, the hunger strike weapon and its effects were discovered by accident and not something thought up as a tactic at a Suffragette headquarters meeting. It was a lone campaigner called Marion Wallace-Dunlop, who was the first to hunger strike and she did it out of frustration and absolutely of her own free will.

Marion, in 1909 was sent to Holloway prison on charges of wilfully and maliciously damaging stonework at the House of Commons. Marion saw herself as a political prisoner, but the prison officials classified her as a 'second division' common criminal inmate. Had she been put into the political prisoner category, then she'd be seen and logged as a 'first division' prisoner… so, in hierarchical terms, Marion felt she'd been undersold… she classed herself as a political prisoner, almost a prisoner of war and so she demanded to be put into the top first division of prisoners! She wasn't, she remained classified as a common criminal and this made her furious. So angry in fact, at her classification, that she decided, much to the surprise of the authorities, the leaders of the Suffragettes, the newspapers and the British public… to go on a hunger strike!

Marion refused to eat anything, until she was reclassified as a political prisoner. She wasn't and so for several days she ate nothing. Increasingly weakening, she was asked by the prison doctor, what she thought she was going to eat to survive… she replied, "My determination".

And determination is something, it was proven, the Suffragettes had in spades!

She would not give in. She constantly refused food and so concerned was the prison governor that Marion might die in her cell of starvation, he decided to release her early. He wanted rid of her, to relinquish any responsibility for this obviously deranged woman!

News spread quickly and immediately other Suffragettes in custody began refusing food and going on hunger strike. This generally, out of fear of anyone dying in custody resulted in the prison authorities releasing the women as soon as they began showing signs of weakness or frailty. Suffragettes then, were being released within a week or so of being put in prison, and to much applause and celebration from their followers when they stepped out of jail. This was a coup for them and disaster for the authorities.

However, it didn't take long before prison life started getting much tougher for the Suffragettes. It was agreed that the judiciary had been far too soft on the women by giving in to their threats of starving themselves to death. It was decided then, that there would be no more early releases for hunger strikers. Now, whether they wanted to be or not, the prisoners would be fed and kept imprisoned. A programme of forced feeding was introduced for any prisoner refusing to eat. Prison wardens, both male and female, held the women down and restrained them, even strapping them to their beds, while medical staff forced greased rubber tubes down the women's throats and up their noses. Then, a mixture of eggs and milk was poured into a funnel and though the tube, directly into the stomach.

This was described at the time as being exceptionally painful and psychologically harrowing... not dissimilar then to being 'water-boarded'.

Any prisoner who fought off the warders during this force feeding, could easily, in the struggle, break their teeth, or cause internal damage, especially in the throat and mouth. This resulted in bleeding, vomiting and on several occasions, as the liquid food, unfortunately made its way into the lungs, close to drowning.

The public were generally outraged by the force-feeding programme and the marketing department at Suffragette headquarters didn't lose any time in producing flyers and posters with images of these poor women going through what could only be described as a torture, at the hands of the British government. Emmeline Pankhurst was incandescent with rage. She described prisons like Holloway in London as being places of horror and torment, with sickening scenes of violence carried out on her fellow Suffragettes. A cynical marketing guru would say this was a coup for the Suffragette movement, because if any in the British public hadn't, up until this point taken too much notice of the vote for women movement, they really could not avoid the subject now… it was splashed all over the newspapers. Support grew even greater for the women throughout the country and abroad, with women in Australia and America in particular, taking inspiration from the British and setting up organisations themselves, based on the Emmeline Pankhurst model.

Public support abroad kept on increasing too for their own Suffragettes and for the British women who were leading the charge. The more the papers carried stories of vulnerable women being mistreated through brutal force feeding, the more the movements around the world grew.

So, if this was a major result in marketing terms for the Suffragettes, it was the exact opposite for the British authorities, who were really, by now, losing control of the situation and had no idea how to deal with it.

In an attempt to turn the tide of public support in their favour, the British Government in 1913 passed an act called the prisoners 'Temporary Discharge for Ill-Health'. This allowed the prison governors to release from jail any hunger striking Suffragette once they'd become too weak to be able to survive without food. So, no more force feeding. The prisoners would simply be allowed to freely starve themselves... almost to death! Then, when it was judged that a particular prisoner was too ill to remain incarcerated, they'd be immediately released from jail and sent home. Once home, they'd be able to recuperate to regain their health and strength. However, this prisoner release programme was only 'on licence' meaning that once back to health and seen again in public, the police would immediately re-arrest the offender and haul them back to jail to serve the remainder of their sentence. At this point, the whole process may well start again. The Suffragette would no doubt go on hunger strike and the authorities would allow her to starve to a certain point, before releasing her again back into the community to recover her health. Once back to full fitness, she'd be re-arrested and jailed. It was an attempt to break the spirit of the hunger strikers and bring the practise to an end. This act of letting prisoners go and then catching them again sometime later, was compared to the game a cat plays with a mouse, so it soon became known in the newspapers and amongst the public as the 'Cat and Mouse Act' And although not as terrible as force feeding prisoners, the act was seen as being very cruel and it certainly didn't win over the majority of the public, which was of course the aim.

Being a hunger striker was, in some quarters akin to being

a war hero. They were celebrated so much in fact that members of the Women's Social and Political Union, who put themselves through a hunger strike in order to further the cause and demand for female votes, were awarded military type campaign medals for doing so. The medals had silver bars which represented periods of hunger strike and enamel bars representing periods of force feeding. The medals were awarded at special breakfast meetings, where leaders of the group handed them out in front of an adoring audience. This was quite an honour and an aspiration for any member of the WSPU.

No Suffragette died in custody during a hunger strike (the authorities made sure of that), although Emmeline Pankhursts' younger sister Mary did die a few days after being released from jail after being subjected to force feeding during her hunger strike. It was claimed that the violence of the force feeding may well have caused a burst blood vessel in her brain, which killed her. Mary was described at the time, as the first martyr to die for the cause. And many women suffered dreadful health problems for the rest of their lives — all caused by the cycle of hunger striking and, in some cases, of course, the consequences of force feeding. Some women died prematurely too, due to complications attributed to their days of hunger striking.

And it wasn't just the ordinary foot soldiers who suffered either. The leaders at the top of the organisation for women's suffrage, genuinely led from the front. Emmeline Pankhurst herself was awarded a hunger strike medal in 1912 after she put herself through the terrible ordeal. This was while serving a two-month sentence for throwing a stone and smashing a window at 10 Downing Street. As well as hunger striking,

Emmeline was also convicted, whilst in prison, of inciting other women to cause criminal and malicious damage to property. In other words, she was grooming them for the outside world... this gained her a further nine months in prison.

Following that, undeterred, Pankhurst continued with her illegal activities and received a three-year sentence of penal servitude. In other words, she was put to hard labour — a terrible punishment and one that, it was hoped, might stop her from being tempted into corrupting other female inmates into her organisation.

The long sentence was for the serious crime of incitement to place an explosive in a building. Pankhurst wasn't the only one to attempt to blow things up either. Many other Suffragettes were doing the same around the country. There were also several occasions when axes were thrown at the passing carriages of MPs on their way to the House of Commons. And an interesting tactic to get their point across was using acids to burn the slogan 'Votes For Women' in huge letters across the greens of the MP's favourite golf courses... this, to many a golf fan at the time (and probably today) was just taking things too far!

But, back to Emmeline. Once in prison for her long and painful stretch, she immediately went on hunger strike and so, as expected, she was released after several days to begin the pattern of 'Cat and Mouse' release, recuperation, re-arrest, hunger strike, release and so on. This went on for a number of months, but she didn't make it easy for the police to re-arrest her!

She travelled around in disguise to avoid detection, went into hiding and even had an all-female Jūjutsu-trained bodyguard to protect her!

The newspapers were full of the saga and finally, the police decided that the negative publicity surrounding this particular case was so great and becoming like a modern-day soap opera, that they, for political and public relations reasons, decided not to re-arrest her... Emmeline beat the system and got off with her three-year stretch of hard labour!

Emmeline Pankhurst is probably the best known of the Suffragettes, due to her being the founder of the organisation and public figurehead of it too, but she's closely followed by another infamous woman, Emily Davison. Infamous in fact for stepping out in front of the King's horse at the 1913 Derby and subsequently killing herself. No one knew she was going to do this, no one knows either, whether it was an attempt to unseat the jockey, pin a 'Votes For Women' badge on the horse, or indeed to commit suicide. She left no note and spoke to no one about her intentions... it's a mystery for sure, but her act that day drew huge public attention to the cause and the injustices women felt at the time. And not only did the event go down in the history books, but when it came to public sympathy, it took the Suffragettes movement to another level.

Prior to that fateful day though, Emily had proven herself, a true militant fighter. She was arrested on nine occasions, went on hunger strike seven times and was force fed forty-nine times.

She'd gained a reputation for her daring deeds of sabotage. She'd set fire to post boxes, smashed windows, thrown stones and even hid in the Palace of Westminster on three occasions. Once, on the night of the 1911 census, she stowed herself away in a broom cupboard in the Palace. This was a clever move, as, the following day, she could record her address on the census as being the 'House of Commons'… because that's where she currently lived — in the broom cupboard! Doing that, she then claimed to have the same political rights as any of the MPs (all male) in the House of Commons, causing no end of embarrassment for them!

A brass plaque, commemorating Emily's overnight stay in the Palace broom cupboard was fitted to the door of it in 1991 by Tony Benn MP. This, strictly speaking was illegal, as Benn had no permission to do so!

At Emily's funeral, a procession of five thousand Suffragettes and their supporters accompanied the coffin and tens of thousands of people lined the route through the streets of London, as the entourage worked its way through the city. The coffin was taken by train to Northumberland, where Emily Davison was buried in her family plot.

There are also plenty of lesser-known Suffragettes, all of whom were great characters with some great stories too. Take Emily Pankhursts' chauffeur of many years as an example. Vera 'Jack' Holme was an actress, a cross-dresser, a singer, and a member of an underground private organisation which she formed with a few other women called the 'Foosack League'. Membership of the organisation was restricted to women only, and especially those who were Suffragettes. The Foosack League by all accounts was a lesbian secret society. Set up at the height of the British Empire and sixty years before homosexuality was decriminalised during the 1960s. This was brave, bearing in mind that just a few years earlier, Oscar Wilde was sentenced to two years hard labour, after being found guilty of indecency and homosexuality. To discover the Foosack League, as one who's membership was restricted to lesbians only, would have been a coup for the authorities at the time and something that would have been hugely detrimental to the Suffragettes and their organisation the WSPU. The scandal would have rocked the foundations of the movement, with sympathetic public figures, organisations and institutions, having no choice but to distance themselves from supporting the Suffragette movement. Cross-dressing chauffeurs and secret lesbian societies would simply be too much to handle for the 'strait-laced' sensibilities and opinions of the day! Public support would have collapsed.

Obviously, drawn to danger, Vera, like Emily Davison, had a reputation for militant behaviour. She once hid overnight in the huge musical organ within Colston Hall in Bristol. Along with another Suffragette, they spent the night inside the instrument and waited for the following day, when local liberal MP Augustine Birrell was to give a speech to an assembled crowd… once the audience were in place and the MP was in full flow, the two women, began bellowing repeatedly from within the organ and invisible to the crowd 'Votes For Women', 'Votes For Women'… the Liberal MP was not amused!

Vera joined the war effort immediately hostilities began in 1914. She became a member of the 'Women's Volunteer Reserve'. This was an organisation that trained female doctors and nurses. Vera employed her chauffeuring skills and became part of the group's transport unit. She served in Serbia and Russia and sometime later was captured by enemy forces and spent a few months imprisoned. Not this time, by the British Government at home, but by the Germans in Austria, as a genuine prisoner of war!

If the Suffragettes weren't out in Europe putting the fear of God into the enemy, then they were at home putting the fear of God into some men in power! These men believed that the women and their militant nature was a danger to society, especially with their increasing anti-social behaviour (including blowing things up, slashing artworks in galleries and setting fire to post boxes) and willingness to use violence to achieve their aims.

In fact, in America at the time, a law was passed to reduce the length of hat pins a lady could wear in her hair, to a maximum six inches. This was because men were becoming increasingly afraid of hat pin wielding, angry and violent Suffragettes!

Hat pins had been popular for some time. The long needle-like pins with decorative stoppers, could be as much as twelve inches in length. The pins held the fashion hats in place, stopping them from being blown off in the wind, or moving about on the head, ruining the set style, which could take hours to achieve.

Stories in the press of ladies fending off male attackers with hat pins were quite normal. Gropers on trains, could easily get a poke in the arm with one, and drunken louts, following ladies around the streets at night, were often sent packing by a hat pin. The readers loved the stories, and the woman were seen as heroes for using their hat pins in self-defence. There was no sympathy for any men injured by a hat pin, if he was acting inappropriately. However, that all changed when the Suffragettes arrived on the scene. Now, stories began appearing in newspapers of wild women, whilst resisting arrests at women's vote marches, attacking police officers with their hat pins. MPs too lived in fear of an approaching Suffragette wearing a particularly large hat!

As for the Americans reducing the legal length of a hat

pin, from twelve inches to six inches. This was quite obviously a sign of desperation and panic, as a six-inch-long needle could do as much damage as a twelve incher!

The fashion of the Suffragette

Don't think for one moment that these women dressed like masculine anarchists, all in black and wearing slightly lopsided berries either… like female versions of Che Guevara! Far from it. The Suffragettes were the exact opposite and exuded style, elegance and celebrated their definite feminine image. This was a directive from the top of the organisation. Suffragettes were encouraged to 'dress themselves in the smartest of clothes'… with so much pressure to look good, many Suffragettes spent more money on clothing than they could afford and were often in debt due to it.

Colours were important too. The leaders of the WSPU as well as the editor of the popular magazine 'Votes For Women' came up with a combination of three colours which represented the organisation and their fight. Effectively, the colours of their flag.

These were green, white and violet (purple) and each colour represented a meaning:

Green for 'Hope'.

White for 'Purity'.

Violet or Purple for 'Loyalty'.

The colours were also popularly used to remind people of what the movement was all about and to ram home the one message the Suffragettes constantly pushed wherever they could… that message and demand was 'give women the vote'. Therefore, take the first letter of each colour and you have G, W and V.

G stands for **give**. W stands for **women** and V stands for **vote**… Give Women the Vote!

Women (and some men) around the world began wearing the Suffragette colours to show their support.

Businesses jumped on board too… this was a fashionable movement to cash in on, so big and well-known companies began lending their support to the cause. Liberty of London, the famous retailer, amongst many others, began selling products from ribbons to badges, jewellery to items of clothing, all in the colours of the Suffragette. This meant that even if you played no part in the campaigning, marching, or hunger striking, you could show your support for the women at the front by buying and wearing the colours of the WSPU.

And talking of being at the front. Hostilities between the WSPU and the British Government were very honourably brought to an end by the Suffragettes at the outset of the First World War. More a ceasefire than a complete ending to be completely correct. The government by now, knew that this group was not going anywhere and would be as determined as before, once the war was over. The WSPU rallied behind the war effort, and they saw it as great opportunity for women to prove themselves as worthy as any man of citizenship and the vote.

Between the years of the war, 1914 to 1918, while the troops were fighting in France, around two million women replaced the men in the factories, workshops and industries around Britain. They not only proved themselves here but became invaluable to the war effort. The combination of this, the years of campaigning before the war and the threat of it reigniting after the war, brought about an act in 1918 which decreed that property owning women over the age of thirty could vote. This was a start and a step in the right direction. Ten years later, in 1928, the age to vote was lowered to twenty-one for both men and women, whether or not they were property owners. Thank the Suffragettes for full British democracy!

Name changes

The German Shepherd dog was a popular choice amongst the pet loving British throughout the empire, but due to the First World War, the breed became unfashionable because of its obvious German roots and connections... owning a German sounding dog was not on, so, cleverly, the dog breeders of the day, changed the name to the 'Alsatian Wolf Dog'. The name struck and the dog's popularity remained. It wasn't until around 1977 that the breed in Britain was again officially recognised as a German Shepherd.

Some families changed their names too. Anyone with a Germanic sounding surname, generally changed to make it more Anglo-Saxon like. This was a sensible move, as anything with a German connection became utterly unacceptable. German products were boycotted. From tin plate toys for children to specialist German beers for adults. They were all no-go areas for the British public. People even began removing the decorative eagles, which often adorned the tops of grandfather clocks. This was in case anyone thought the owner might be a secret supporter of the Kaiser!

The most famous British family to do a quick name change was the Saxe-Coburg-Gotha's, who in 1917 changed theirs to 'Windsor'... as in the house of Windsor... the Royal family!

Jokes from the British Empire. Now you'll understand where the Christmas cracker jokes come from!

Why is a dog like a tree? Because they both lose their bark once they're dead.

'How did you make it up with your wife?'

'As usual, I apologised for being right'.

'A burglar got into the house of a lawyer the other day… after a terrible struggle, the lawyer succeeded in robbing him'.

Who is the greatest chicken-killer in Shakespeare? Macbeth, because he did murder most foul.

Why should the number 288 never be mentioned in company? Because it is two gross.

Note: *A gross is a dozen x dozen (144) This was a common measurement at the time.*

"There's a man at Camberwell so fat that they grease the omnibus-wheels with his shadow."

Anxious wife to doctor: "Doctor, how is my husband?"

Doctor: "He will survive. What he needs now is peace and quiet. I have here a couple of opiates."

Wife: "When shall I give them to him?"

Doctor: "Madam, they are for you. Your husband needs rest."

"Doesn't it make you dizzy to waltz?"

"Yes, but one must get used to it, you know. It's the way

of the whirled."

Pawnbrokers prefer customers without any redeeming qualities.

When a man wants to learn to play the cornet, it is only natural that he should engage a tooter!

Why is a manuscript always called a MS? Because that is the state in which the editor finds it.

A lady wrote the following letters at the bottom of her flour barrel: O I C U R M T.

Why is the devil riding a mouse like one and the same thing? Because it's synonymous.

"Do you think you could love me, Maud?"

"I don't know Algernon, I might. I learnt German once."

Herbert has named his horse, 'Sensitive', because he takes a fence so easily.

After a man has trodden barefoot on a tack, the family parrot has to be kept out of the room when the minister calls.

Many a man makes a good reputation on what is not found out about him.

Clever Dogs and Bank Holidays

You can thank the banker, author, philanthropist, scientist and campaigner for workers' rights, Sir John Lubbock for the bank holidays you enjoy today... and no doubt, take for granted!

As well as the above, Sir John was also a politician who was keen to improve the daily conditions for Britain's millions of workers who toiled away in the new industrialised and revolutionised 24/7 factories. These places made the desirable products that were shipped around the colonies and indeed the rest of the world... all of which generated huge profits for Britain and her empire.

In 1871, he proposed an idea to parliament of regular and extra days off for workers. Days, when the financial institutions would be closed too, giving bank workers some much need time off too. The extra holidays would always be on a Monday, so the British workers could enjoy a 'long weekend'. Sir John argued that this would give employees more time with their families and also the time to enjoy such things as trips to the beach, the zoo, to play cricket, or take picnics to the park. All of which would be beneficial to, not only the workers, but also the economy, with a happier, healthier, and more productive workforce. An all-round winning idea then. Parliament agreed and the 'Bank Holiday Act' was passed in 1871 to much celebration around the county.

Descriptions of the very first bank holiday in 1871 make

interesting reading. The country, according to news reports went 'slightly mad'. So many people flocked to the seaside, to the parks and rivers that paddle steamers almost sank with the amount of people on board, trains bulged at the seams and crowds jostled and argued on the station platforms to get aboard. Extra Omnibuses were put on, but still they overflowed with passengers travelling across towns to visit friends and relatives. One steamer boat on the Thames, after a journey down the river, packed with celebratory holidaymakers, was unable to dock at Margate, its final destination, due to hundreds of fellow holidaymakers crammed onto the jetty there. Disembarking would have been too dangerous, so it had to turn around!

The morning and afternoon of the first bank holiday was bad enough with hundreds of thousands of people moving from one location to another. However, it got a bit rowdier, later on in the day, when the crowds were all heading home… a high percentage of whom had spent their extra day off in one tavern or another!

Newspapers dubbed Sir John Lubbock the most popular man in the country and for some years after the first bank holiday was introduced, the extra days off, were known as 'St Lubbock's Days'!

Sir John was a great animal and insect lover — he kept pet wasps and ants at home to study and was known to carry bees in his briefcase. This fact came as a shock to a thief one day, after he stole Sir John's case, opened it up, saw the bees and quickly closed it again before abandoning the idea of pinching the case… which was soon returned to its owner. On another occasion, carrying ferrets in his briefcase, Sir John lost some important parliamentary documents… the ferrets ate all his papers!

He carried out experiments on his ants to test their intelligence, which he was highly impressed by. He discovered that if he gave a few drops of alcohol to half of the ants, they'd soon get rolling drunk... so much so, that they were unable to walk. He was amazed to witness then, the other half of the colony (the sober ones) picking up the drunkards and carrying them back home to the safety of the nest... not unlike the very first bank holiday!

Sir John was convinced that one of his dogs, a puppy called Van, was so intelligent he could teach him to read!

So, he began by covering the dog's food bowl with a piece of card, with the word 'food' written on it. In order for Van to get fed, he was trained to bring the food card to his master. After several weeks of this, Sir John hid the dog bowl and offered Van a selection of cards to look at instead. Each card had a different word written on it, including the one marked with 'food'. In order to be fed, Van needed to choose the food card... which he always did. Then, the puppy learnt the same for 'water' and for 'bone'. Of course, being a sophisticated dog, Van also loved a nice cup of tea, so in order to get one, he was trained to bring the card marked 'tea' to Sir John!

So clever was Van, that when he wanted to be let out into the garden, he brought a card in his mouth to Sir John, which read 'out'.

On one occasion, when the dog was feeling ill and off colour, when offered varying cards, he refused to choose the 'food' card until he was feeling a little better, proving to Sir John that the dog could indeed read!

Popular names during the British Empire (NOTE: Names need tidying up. E.g. Gwendoline — Wilhelmina)

For boys

Albert
Alfred
Algernon
Ambrose
Archibald
Arthur
Aubrey
Augustine
Augustus
Basil
Bernard
Bertram
Cecil
Cedric
Clarence
Claude
Clement
Clifford
Cornelius
Cuthbert
Cyril
Donald
Douglas
Duncan

Enoch
Eugene
Eustace
Evan
Ernest
Ebenezer
Ewart
Edgar
Edwin
Edmund
Edward
Felix
Fergus
Francis
Frank
Franklin
Frederick
Geoffrey
George
Gerald
Gilbert

Harold
Harvey
Herbert
Herman
Horace
Howard
Hugh
Hugo
Humphrey
Ivan
Ivor Jasper
Jonathan
Julian
Julius
Kenneth
Laurence
Leonard
Leopold
Leslie
Malcolm
Maurice
Maxwell
Miles
Montague
Neville
Nigel
Oliver
Oscar
Owen

Percival
Percy
Philip
Ralph
Randolph
Raymond
Reginald
Reuben
Roderick
Roger
Rupert
Rufus
Septimus
Sidney
Silas
Simeon
Stanley
Theodore
Timothy
Valentine
Vernon
Victor
Vincent
Walter
Wilfred

For girls

Ada	Edith	Ida	Mercy
Adelaide	Eliza	Isabel	Mildred
Adeline	Ellen	Irene	Millicent
Agatha	Elsie	Iris	Minnie
Agnes	Emmeline	Ivy	Olive
Alice	Ethel	Kate	Patience
Amelia	Eugenie	Kathleen	Phoebe
Amy	Eva	Jemima	Phyllis
Annie	Eveline	Jenny	Priscilla
Augusta	Fanny Flora	Jessie	Prudence
Beatrice	Florence	Josephine	Rhoda
Blanche	Frances	Julia	Rosa
Cecilia	Freda	Lavinia	Rose
Cecily	Georgina	Leah	Rosetta
Clara	Gertrude	Lillian	Rosina
Clarissa	Gladys	Lily	Ruby
Clementina	Grace	Louisa	Selina
Constance	Gwendoline	Lucy	Susannah
Cora	Harriet	Lydia Mabel	Sylvia
Cordelia	Helen	Margaret	Tabitha
Daisy	Helena	Marguerite	Theodora
Delia	Henrietta	Marjorie	Theresa
Dorcas	Hetty	Martha	Ursula
Doris	Hilda	Matilda	Victoria
Dorothy	Honor	Maude / Maud	Violet
		May	Wilhelmina
			Winifred

Terrible Empire Jobs

Toshers, Mud Larks, Grubbers and Body Finders!
London in particular had thousands of sewer hunters, also known as 'Toshers'. They searched day and night for anything of value, discarded or thrown away. During the 19th century, with the quickly growing empire, its capital city was also expanding — in fact, it was positively bulging at the seams. In the hundred years from 1800 to 1900, London's population grew from one million to six million. London was the biggest city in the world and not only the capital of the empire, but the worlds capital for trade, finance and new inventions… the high-tech hub of the world.

You can imagine then, the pull this cosmopolitan city had on anyone wanting to make a name for themselves, make their fortune, to better themselves, or just find a highly paid job. London was the Hollywood of the world, and anything it was believed was possible, if you moved to London… people, full of hope and expectations flocked to London… most were dashed!

Mind you, it wasn't just London. Other cities' populations exploded around Britain. The industrial revolution, with all its benefits, also came at a cost to the more traditional methods of making a living out in the countryside. Therefore, agricultural workers and those working in the small cottage industry type businesses far away from the cities, began migrating to the swelling metropolis.

Then, as now, life wasn't quite as easy as people had hoped once they'd moved to London. Many a dream was shattered by the hard realities of city life and with no government benefit system to fall back on, large numbers of workers were forced to do whatever they could to make ends meet. It probably goes without saying, that crime was a huge problem for anyone living in a city.

Overcrowding, dreadful sanitation, terrible working conditions and low pay, all contributed to the term invented in the 19th century to describe the poor workers who toiled away, merely to survive in the dark, dingy, and dangerous city streets. They were called for obvious reasons… 'The Great Unwashed'.

If you couldn't find work and you didn't fancy robbing people in the street or breaking into houses and risking going to jail for a very long time doing hard labour, one option was to go down, deep into the city sewers and become a 'Tosher'. You'd be armed with a scarf across your face (to keep the smell out) a stick for poking around (and defending yourself) a candle or two and a bag or a basket to collect any found treasure! Then, you'd have everything you need to be able to scavenge around in the murky, foul waters of London's sewers. Down there could be found all sorts of things that could be sold to pay rent and buy food. Items that had been mistakenly thrown or flushed from above into the sewer system for any waiting Tosher!

Toshers hunted in the dark, or at best dim light of the sewers. Conditions were as bad as you can possibly imagine. Rats the size of cats, killer diseases, other competing Toshers and sewer gases were all waiting for you… all of them could quite easily do you some serious harm, or as often happened, kill you!

A lucky Tosher would be one that found a gold coin, a lost ring, or just a piece of unburnt coal. An unlucky Tosher, would be one who fell foul of any of the dangers mentioned above, or the common and great fear of taking a wrong turning in the maze of the sewer system and getting lost, deep below the streets of London… never to be seen again!

In London, the empire's capital, the river Thames was effectively an open sewer and a drain for industrial waste. It was a highway for trade too of course, with a huge amount of river traffic running up and down it twenty-four hours a day. There were also hundreds of quays dotted along its banks and the activity here was constant. Loading and unloading of goods and products from all around the world employed thousands of people working along the river's shores. The place hummed with activity, not all of it legal and a lot of it quite dodgy. It also attracted plenty of undesirable characters. This was a very rough place to live and work!

Looking at the river today, it's hard to envisage just how overcrowded it was during this time, but the Thames was a far busier place than you can possibly imagine. It also smelt worse than you can possibly imagine. In fact, the whole of London, partly due to the open sewer of the river, stank to high heaven!

And if all of this doesn't yet sound like an image from hell, then consider this: It shouldn't come as a big surprise to learn that it was a common sight to see dead bodies floating up and down the river mixing in with and getting in the way of all the river traffic!

Suicides, murder victims, drunks falling overboard and

over bridges (alcoholism was very normal at this time), all added to the number of 'floaters' found in the river. But, like most things in life, there's often an upside to something that on the surface seems negative. The upside here was because of the number of dead bodies in the river, there was good employment for a group of people called the 'Thames Body Finders'! Yes, it was their job to find and fish out the bodies. They'd use grappling hooks and large nets to drag the bodies on board their rowing boat, which they'd use to scour the river for the potentially lucrative floaters! And they could be lucrative too. If the dead body belonged to someone who was actually missed and liked by family or friends, there would be a reward for the finding and returning of it. On the other hand, if no one claimed the body, or it was unrecognisable, then there would be no money in it for the body finders. That was just the nature of their business. You win some, you lose some. However, there was always the hope that the corpse might have about its person some valuables. A watch and chain maybe, or better still some cash. The bodies would be stripped clean of anything of value, before being handed over to relatives… no body was ever returned with any valuables — that was just the accepted bonus for being a Body Finder!

Similar to the Toshers who worked below ground, were the 'Mud Larks' who worked above it. Mud Larks searched along the banks of muddy rivers at low tide. They'd be looking for anything that might have fallen overboard from a trading boat, or an item of value accidentally thrown away and lost amongst the sewage. People often washed their clothes in rivers, so items of clothing would regularly turn up in the most surprising of places too. These could easily be dried out and sold on.

This work wasn't quite as dangerous an occupation, as being underground, but Mud Larks were possibly even more susceptible to disease, than the Toshers. They'd often cut themselves on broken glass and pottery, as they rummaged through the mud and with the river waters being so filthy dirty and full of human waste, rubbish, dead cats and dogs, the regular cuts they suffered to their legs, feet and hands could easily turn sceptic. And it wasn't just dead animals the Mud Larks encountered either. Any bodies the Body Finders had missed would eventually turn up on a river bank somewhere… to be picked over by the Mud Larks!

Mud Larks had a reputation for pilfering and so the general population kept a close eye on them, as they wandered along the riverbanks in search of anything to sell. Homeowners nearby needed to be vigilant, as did passing river traffic if Mud Larks were around!

During this period, if you didn't fancy going into the dark sewers, or getting soaked every day along the river, then you could always become a 'Grubber'. Grubbers worked the drainage systems in the streets and throughout the cities, catching anything of value, before it disappeared below ground and headed on, in the direction of a Tosher!

Tannery Workers and Pure Finders

Leather tanning was big business during the boom years of the empire. Leather was a product in much demand around the world and British Leathers were amongst some of the finest available.

If you've ever been unfortunate enough to visit a tannery, you'll remember the terrible stench of it. The smell is overpowering and nauseating — it's quite foul and unlike anything else you'll experience. Even though workers and nearby residents at the time soon grew accustomed to the aroma (many were born into the business) anyone visiting a place near a tannery, soon moved on!

Skins arrived at the factory, dried and caked in dirt, blood and pieces of rotting flesh. These were cleaned in vats of water and noxious chemicals, before being scraped by hand to remove any unwanted bits, and then the skins were put into another vat. This time not only did the vat contain horrible chemicals, but it was mixed with large quantities of urine! The leather was left to soak for a while in the solution, which loosened any stubborn, left-over hairs. These were finally scraped off by a tanner using a large double handled tool with a sharp edge, which was especially designed for the job. And it was a messy job. Wet, sludgy, and foul!

The process of preparing the skins and turning them into fine leathers for clothing, saddles, sofas, or shoes then was long, laborious and very, very smelly!

And talking of smells, here comes the worst bit. To give the leather the softness, that the end consumer, the world over, demanded, the hides needed a further treatment called 'bating'. To bate a hide was to rub vigorously into it a solution of water, chemicals, and the most crucial element… dog poo. Apparently, the bacteria found in this ingredient was just the job for softening up leather!

You can imagine then that the workers in the tanneries themselves developed a smell that was impossible to disguise. It became part of their very fibre. They, their homes, and the surrounding area became impregnated with the whiff of the tannery, so you found that most leather workers lived and socialised together, within their own communities, far away from other people with nicer, less smelly jobs… bearing in mind, that most tannery workers went weeks without bathing (apart from unintentionally at work!) they were not overly popular due to their aroma, beyond the periphery of the leather factory!

Some people, who were not employees of the tanneries did willingly visit the factories though, and on a regular basis. In fact, as often as they possibly could… these were the self-employed 'Pure Finders'.

A pure finder was a hunter, scavenger, collector, and supplier of the much sought after, fresh dog poo to a tannery! Their job was to scour the city streets in search of the commodity, collect and then deliver it to the leather factories. The factories couldn't get enough of it, so it wasn't a bad business if you could find a good supply of the stuff!

Dogs were particularly popular pets, just as they are today and owners then, luckily for the pure finders, were not as conscientious as they are now with picking up their dog's droppings and putting it into designated bins. No, it was simply left all over the place, free for anyone who fancied scooping it up. City streets were also filled with feral dogs, so the supply was pretty plentiful for anyone willing to get out there and collect it for the leather tanners. Some pure finders were even known to follow and stalk dog walkers around parks in the hope their dog might provide an extra bit of income!

Not so bad jobs

A Funeral Mute

It was quite usual during the 19th century to hold extraordinarily large funerals. Even people who could barely afford it, spent all their savings, plus borrowings on extravagant affairs when it came to burying their loved ones. Funeral savings plans were all the rage and families would religiously pay into them for years, forgoing any luxury and even food just to keep up the payments!

The alternative to not having enough money for a good funeral when the time came, was the dreaded pauper's burial. This would be reluctantly paid for by the state (not that the cost was high!) and would involve the departed being put into a communal grave, with as many as a dozen or more other paupers. No headstone and no religious ceremony either. The idea of any of this filled everyone with horror. And the next bit of information will fill you with horror too. It was not uncommon in the sections of graveyard where paupers were buried, due to there being so many of them in one grave, for parts of bodies to start poking out through the earth. It gets worse. Grave diggers sometimes had to stamp on the bodies to push them back underground again!

So, the bigger the funeral service someone received, the greater the importance was attached to that person and their lives… as well as the family arranging the burial. It was an opportunity for the relatives to show the world how successful they were and very often, more money was spent on people when they were dead, than when they were alive!

Social pressure, to give someone a big 'send off', was huge within all communities and a big funeral was an indicator that the family were high up the social ladder, no matter where on the social scale they were. The bigger and grander the affair, the more credibility the living members of the family would get in their community. Therefore, it was not uncommon to see, driving through even the poorest of neighbourhoods, a new impressive design of hearse that appeared during the mid-19th century. These were seriously flash affairs. Coach built in mahogany, intricately carved and painted in black, with silver and gold enhancements. The sides of the vehicle were designed to be almost all glass, so the coffin and the bulging flower arrangements were on full view. This meant that all the mourners and the by-standers could get a good look at the 'no expense' spared solid oak coffin, with chunky elaborate and expensive brass handles. Watching funerals was a popular and fascinating pastime, so there would always be a decent crowd! Of course, the hearse would be pulled by horses. Two was the minimum required to tug such a weighty carriage, but as you'd expect, the more horses and the more expensive, the better! Extra horses were costly 'add ons' so, to do it right, four horses would be better and six of the blighters would be fabulous… and far more impressive!

The horses were decked out in fine regalia, including plumes of highly expensive ostrich feathers. The number of plumes per horse would be noted by the observant crowd too. These were another indicator as to the wealth and status of the deceased. Two plumes were usual per horse, four was better, but seven plumes of ostrich feathers indicated that the deceased and their family were seriously loaded!

All black, or all white horses were available. Black ones were the most popular, but on busy days, when there were no black horses available, the funeral director was always able to dye the white horses, black!

All in all, a funeral was a seriously expensive and important affair — but, it could easily set a family back years, financially speaking. People would forgo all sorts of life's luxuries, treats and even necessities like clothing and food, just to put on a 'good funeral'.

Another added expense was the daily fee of a Funeral Mute. A mute was a paid mourner. It would be unlikely that anyone at the funeral would know him, but that didn't matter, he was there to look as solemn as possible and being called a mute, he wasn't allowed to talk to anyone either.

Good mutes were those that had a natural and unfortunately miserable and melancholic look to them. They were the most sought after. There was absolutely no point in employing a mute with a jolly, sparkly disposition!

Being a mute was often a part time job, so most would be something like day labourers, working when they could. One day brick laying, or cleaning windows, the next being a mute.

This was a zero hours work system and people needed to be able to turn their hands to whatever work was available.

The mute work was probably the best paid and easiest of all their jobs, however. They'd be dressed all in black of course, with a large top hat and their job would entail keeping vigil outside the house of the deceased and then, when the time came, to lead the funeral procession of the horse-drawn hearse from the front... looking as miserable as possible!

A big upside to being a mute, apart from the pay, which wasn't bad, was the free alcohol. It was customary to give the mute a shot of gin every now and then, especially if it was cold outside, as they were keeping vigil. Mutes though, because of this, developed a terrible reputation for drinking far too much and getting positively drunk... this, if you think about it, is highly unprofessional at a funeral!

Mutes became so synonymous with drunken behaviour that officials at the 'Burial Society' were quoted in magazines and newspapers complaining about the behaviour of mutes. They claimed that mutes were often seen staggering around in the road, so drunk they couldn't walk in a straight line (and this was in front of the funeral procession). Some mutes, after the funeral service was over, even needed to be driven home in the back of a hearse, as they were so inebriated that they were incapable of walking... ironically, they were described as being 'dead drunk'!

So, being a mute wasn't a bad job at all... and in London, in 1854, it got even better. Mutes began enjoying day trips away. Away from the smog, grime, and smelly streets of London — out into the fresh air of the countryside.

In November 1854, the 'London Necropolis Railway' was opened. The train line was specifically constructed to carry dead bodies and mourners between London and a newly opened cemetery, located far away from the overcrowded burial grounds of London and to the peace and quiet of the country. It was twenty-three miles southwest of the city in Brookwood, Surrey. The Brookwood cemetery was huge. In fact, when it was opened, it was instantly the largest of its kind, anywhere in the world. And it needed to be — the population of London had more than doubled in the fifty odd years since the beginning of the 19th century. The cemetery was so big in fact, that it was designed to be large enough to accommodate all the deaths in London for hundreds of years to come.

This then was a very impressive operation, but it was also a serious commercial venture with shareholders and investors to tempt in and to placate with financial rewards. There's money in death and this was a huge potential money maker... the directors of the company knew this and fortunately for them, people in London were dying regularly from all sorts of dreadful diseases and complaints. From malnutrition to dysentery, drownings to mysterious murders. All these bodies needed burying, and the London Necropolis Company catered literally for every dead body in London!

It didn't matter whether the person was rich, poor, from high society or from low, there was a burial option for all!

The plots in the cemetery were priced on a sliding scale. A good location, with the right to erect a permanent monument to the deceased would be at the top end of the price list. This was very desirable if the family could afford it and the location ensured that the dead person's neighbours were of a similar social sort too... therefore, the family were guaranteed that there would be no riff-raff buried nearby! So, in death, as in life, the residents of London were segregated from one another by social status and wealth. The rich in one area and the poor in another.

Even the railway station waiting rooms and the compartments on the train, were divided into first-, second- and third-class compartments. This applied, not only the passengers, as in the mourners en route to the cemetery, but even to the coffin carriages — they too were divided into classes. This prevented any cross-contamination and unpleasantness by keeping different sections of society away from one another!

With the massive growth in London's infrastructure, the civil engineering projects were often held up by dozens of old burial grounds, which were getting in the way of development. These cemeteries needed to be moved to make way for new train stations, roads, hotels, sewers and of course the new underground railway.

Luckily, Brookwood opened at the perfect time for London's expansion. It was ideally suited as a place to house the bodies London needed to dispose of. The first major relocation of ancient bodies was in 1862, with the construction of Charring Cross station, where around eight thousand bodies were crated up in batches of twenty-six and sent by rail on the Necropolis Line to Brookwood for re-burial… this, no doubt was an added bonus for the directors of the cemetery!

So, there is no doubt about it. The empire builders spent a lot of effort, time, thought and cash on their funerals. They planned them years in advance, put aside money they could barely afford and went without luxuries in life, all to pay for something they would never see, or experience!

Not so much is spent on funerals today, but the closest equivalent to the potential financial ruination of a family, is the modern wedding ceremony! The Victorians spent more money on death, than they did the celebration of two people sharing a life together, but we in the 21st century often spend far too much money (we don't have) on weddings, to impress people who don't care, don't matter or don't know us... not much really changes!

As happy as a Sandboy!

Now here's a saying that everyone must have heard before... if you're pleased with yourself, something's gone well, or you've had a particularly good day, you could be described as being, 'as happy as a sandboy'.

Sandboys were employed by taverns and inns to collect fresh buckets of sand on a daily basis, drag them into the tavern and sprinkle the stuff onto the floor of the bar. Not dissimilar to how butchers used to spread sawdust on their floors to soak up the blood, the pubs used sand to soak up all the spilt beers, ales, gin, and spit! The sand kept the stone floors from being slippy and therefore this cut down on nasty drunken accidents.

Each morning, the old sand from the night before was shovelled up and dumped, before a fresh sprinkling was added. All of this was the sandboy's responsibility and, excitingly, every morning he'd get the chance to sieve through the old, soaked sand before he disposed of it. In the sieving, he'd be hoping to find lost coins, watch chains, pipes, snuff boxes, or anything a drunken reveller the night before might have mislaid during a particularly heavy drinking session... anything he did find, he could keep. That was the deal the sandboys had with the pub owners. As well as this though, the sandboy was paid for his work in cash and in beer... the daily supply of alcohol kept him merry in his work, whilst he searched for treasure in the sand... who wouldn't be 'as happy as a sandboy'?

Unusual job titles and descriptions — from the period of the British Empire

Advertisement conveyancer… a man who walks around wearing an advertising sandwich board

Aeronaut… a balloonist or trapeze artist

Ale Wife… a landlady of a tavern

Amen Man… parish clerk

Bagniokeeper… a person who runs a bathhouse or a brothel

Bang Beggar… an officer of the parish who controls the stay of any visiting stranger

Belly Builder… maker and fitter of piano interiors

A Bender… person who cuts leather

Bumboat Man… someone who sells wares to ship's crews and passengers, once they've docked

Chanty Man… a sailor who led the songs on board ship

Cow Leech… and animal doctor

Deathsman… an executioner

Domesman… a judge

Drugger… a chemist

Executrix… a female executioner

Fripperer… buyer and seller of old clothes

Funambulist… a tightrope walker

Guinea Pig… an odd job man whose fee was usually a guinea

Knockknobbler… someone who catches stray dogs

Long Song Seller… someone who sold songsheets of popular songs, usually about a yard long

Potato Badger… a potato seller

Quarrel Picker… a window glazer

Sawbones… a surgeon

Soap Licker… maker of soap

Toe Rag… a porter in the docks

Town Husband… someone who is paid to collect money from fathers of illegitimate children for their upkeep

Vaginarious… a sheath or scabbard maker

The first underground train line in the world (The Tube)

The British built the first ever passenger railway in the world. Opened in 1825, the track known as The Stockton to Darlington Railway paved the way for trains to change the way the rest of the world moved its goods and its people safely and efficiently... and forever.

The first underground award also goes to the British. In 1863 The Metropolitan Underground railway in London was opened and on its first day of business, it carried thirty-eight thousand eager and excited passengers, all of whom experienced something no one else in the world had ever experienced... underground travel. Some also experienced a new form of travel sickness!

Long before electric or diesel engines were introduced, the only way to haul passengers and trade goods below the streets of London in 1863 was to use the same trains they were using above ground... steam trains!

Gas lit wooden carriages were pulled by locomotives which understandably belched out noxious fumes, just as they did above ground. Fumes here though, had nowhere go — other than to fill the dark tunnels with huge quantities of thick black smoke and dust.

Passengers were advised then to keep all windows tightly shut to stop the smoke from entering the carriage. However, draft excluding wasn't quite what it is today, and the fumes, sulphur and coal dust soon found its way into the carriages. Mix that with the heat, the smell of burning oil lamps, cigarette and pipe smoke, as well as tightly packed passengers and you have a nightmare concoction.

In this atmosphere, some people collapsed, and hundreds complained of feeling as though they were going to die of asphyxiation! Many more predicted that the underground railway would soon be discontinued on health grounds.

But on the other hand, and quite bizarrely, some people firmly believed that travelling on the underground railway could well be beneficial to your health, if you suffered from a number of diseases, or complaints. These included, asthma, bronchitis, tonsillitis and even anorexia!

The directors of the railway knew that the air conditioning system needed to be improved and this happened over time. They tried all sorts of things, from garden plants in carriages and at stations to conductors and other train staff being encouraged to grow beards, as these, it was believed, would help to clean the air by acting as filters!

From around 1890, electric powered trains were introduced… again, the British were the first to run electric trains!

Electric cars

Keeping on the subject of electricity. This was a power source that was far from being new. Electricity had been used for well over a hundred years on all sorts of applications, from experimental transport to electric shock treatments for health and even pleasure purposes (read my previous book 'A Romp with The Georgians')!

In around 1832, Scotsman, Robert Anderson developed the first crude electric vehicle. Powered by a non-rechargeable battery, it wasn't exactly efficient, but electricity certainly played a fundamental part in the development of the motor vehicle.

Motor cars were a common site from around 1890. These were a mix of petrol, steam and electric powered. By 1900, it's estimated that over one third of all cars sold were electric!

The combustion engine had a longer range than the electric version, although it was criticised for pumping out pollution and dreadful noise. It was also a bone shaker with its vibration caused by the heavy petrol driven engine... the driver and passengers also had to endure sucking in the fumes and potentially arriving at their final destination with their faces and clothing covered in oil, soot, and mucky radiator water!

The electric car, on the other hand, had a much lower range, due to problems with battery storage and size (some things don't change!) but it was far cleaner and emitted barely any noise whatsoever. Electric cars were preferred for city use, where the fact that they had a low range wasn't as important. They were much easier to drive too, being far smoother and with no gear changes required. Advertisements at the time promised that within twenty minutes, any new owner could be on the road handling the machine perfectly well! The makers particularly promoted their electric car towards women and although they proved popular with female drivers, it meant that many men were put off from owning an electric vehicle… it was seen as being a bit of a 'girly' car! In an attempt to attract male buyers, electric car makers started adding massive fake radiators to the fronts of the vehicle to give the impression they were really quite butch, petrol driven vehicles!

In 1897, Taxi drivers, were quite obviously secure in their sexuality, as in London, there was a fleet of electric cabs that buzzed about the streets, morning and night, almost silently… they just emitted a very low humming noise and the cars, because of this, gained the nickname, 'The Hummingbirds'.

Electric car sales peaked around 1910, but soon after and with big improvements in their engineering, petrol driven vehicles began to be more popular. Mufflers were designed to reduce the racket the machines made, more modern engines could travel even further, and road infrastructure improvements meant that long distance travel by motor car was easy and fast. Plus, the fact that large reserves of crude oil were being discovered around the world, the petrol needed to power the vehicles became far cheaper… the poor electric car just couldn't compete and so, soon after became just obsolete… that is, until today!

Rolls-Royce

You can't talk about motor cars from this period without mentioning the world's most famous and highly regarded car brand, Roll-Royce. A true product of the British Empire, the company was founded by Charles Rolls and Henry Royce.

Henry Royce established an electrical and mechanic business in 1884, and in 1904 he built his first car. This car, he sold through top end dealers and one car dealer he got along particularly well with was Charles Rolls. They became business colleagues as well as friends and the combination of the two characters, with Rolls' marketing and selling skills, mixed with Royce's engineering abilities, they felt, was the perfect partnership. So, in 1906, the pair made an agreement where Henry Royce would now build motor cars which would be sold exclusively by Charles Rolls... no other dealers were able to sell these vehicles and the new models would be retailed under the brand name of Rolls-Royce.

Some would say that the pair were unusual bedfellows. Royce coming from a working-class background, leaving school and beginning work at the age of nine. By fourteen, he was an apprentice on the railways and it was here that his genius as an engineer was discovered. Royce funded himself to go to night school where he studied the basics, as well as electrical engineering, and soon set up his own business making and selling new designs in electrical doorbells and dynamos. After buying his first second-hand car, a French Decauville, he began effectively taking it apart and discovering design and construction faults, he vowed he could do better... he built his first engine in 1903 and the first 'Royce' car was on the road in 1904, hence the meeting with Charles Rolls.

Having found construction faults in the French Decauville, Royce vowed to do better. By the end of 1903, he had designed and built his first petrol engine — and in April 1904, he drove his first Royce 10hp motor car into town.

The Silver Ghost was launched in that year, and it was soon described by motoring journalists as 'the best car in the world'… being the best meant it was also one of the most expensive in the word and this attracted the super wealthy motoring fans. They wanted the very finest machine on offer, and they flocked to order their Rolls-Royce. It's no different today. There probably isn't an Oligarch in the world without a Rolls-Royce in his collection, and the same applied to the uber rich in the early years of the 20th century. The Oligarchs then though, were certainly not Russian… they were Indian… enter the fabulously wealthy and equally egocentric Indian Kings, the Maharajahs!

The kings of India first fell in love with Rolls-Royce in 1907 when the company sent a Silver Ghost on a six-hundred-and-twenty-mile trial between Bombay and Kolhapur. The arduous journey through several mountain passes proved that the luxury brand not only looked stunning, elegant and stylish, but was highly reliable, tough and capable. For Indian royalty, a Rolls-Royce suddenly represented the ultimate expression of wealth and power, and everyone wanted one! By the early 1920s, Rolls-Royce had established showrooms in Bombay, Calcutta and Delhi, making it handy for any prince to nip along to his local showroom! By then, around one in five new Roll-Royce motor cars were shipped to India. Most Maharajahs owned several of the brand, some dozens — the average was

3.5 Rolls-Royce cars per Maharajah, with the Maharajah of Patiala owning forty-four!

The majority of Roll-Royce buyers in Europe and America opted for their coach-built bodies to be refined, sophisticated, even understated. They were big and bold by nature, but most purchasers wanted such a vehicle to give the impression of a cultured owner. In other words, the rich self-made mill owner from Lancashire could at sixty miles an hour, pass as an aristocrat!

This idea of social climbing meant nothing to the Maharajahs… they were at the top of the tree and had nothing to prove to anyone. They were free to do as they wished with their cars, anything went and they created some, what can only be described as magnificent, works of art on wheels. As with all art though, it is of course, subjective!

To match their palaces, clothing and lifestyle, some of the Indian super rich demanded and specified opulent, outrageous, and eccentric embellishments for their cars. They blinged them up beyond belief! Special paint effects of course (one prince sent his wife's pink slipper in the post to Roll-Royce for them to colour match it for his new car) along with family crests and mottos, but also gold and silver plating, jewel and ivory inlays, elaborate interior lighting, massive drinks cabinets, beds, huge spotlights, even bigger horns and many had gun-racks fitted for tiger hunting parties in the jungle. And if the princes were serious about going hunting, they had machine guns mounted to do the job properly!

Some cars were so heavily bejewelled with diamonds and rubies that they needed armed guards to watch over them during visits to the garage for servicing or repairs!

One teetotal Indian ruler ordered a Rolls-Royce especially for his wife (who definitely wasn't teetotal). The vehicle was fitted out with a bar and with matching crystal decanters and glasses. This was described as her 'drinking car'. Another had a special stool fitted in front of where his wife sat. This was especially made for a dwarf servant, whose job it was to massage the Maharani's legs, when she went on a long journey!

The term 'passion wagon' is a late 20th century one and might describe a flash car, driven around to impress a partner, or even jokingly, an old van, kitted out as a hippy camper.

The term though aptly describes the most exotic of all the Maharajah cars. This was an exuberant and hugely costly Rolls-Royce convertible with a reputation for being a proper passion wagon! The vehicle was silver plated and drop dead gorgeous — it was believed to emit amazing, spiritually stimulating (and otherwise) waves from its coach work. These waves had the ability in which to woo any passenger or passer-by — the driver wished! The special car was even lent out to other princes on their wedding nights… a guaranteed Viagra tablet on wheels! It wasn't just the Maharaja's who were trying to outdo one another with their outrageous personally designed motor cars either.

In Calcutta, the capital of British India during the early part of the 20th century lived an eccentric and exceptionally wealthy Scotsman and car lover named Robert Nicholl Matthewson who went by the slightly unimaginative nickname 'Scotty'!

Scotty Matthewson wanted to show off to the local Calcutta elite and shock the cities inhabitants with his very own modified car.

He did more than impress the local Maharaja's though — he terrified half the population with his outrageous vehicle.

Called the 'Swan Car' the machine genuinely looked like a swan gliding through water! The car's coachwork in fact was modelled on the body of a swan, or rather an interpretation of one! Amber coloured electric light bulbs glowed from its eyes, almost frightening to death most people who saw it coming at them at night. And the experience would have been made even worse if 'Scotty' blew the swans horn... this was operated from the back seat, where he'd be relaxing — the multi sounds it made was terrifyingly loud (it even played tunes).

The sight and sound of the beast on wheels certainly cleared the road of pedestrians, but if people got too close to the swan, maybe whilst driving through the city centre, then the driver could spray steam out of the bird's beak to scare anyone off the road ahead!

Brushes were fitted to the tyres to sweep away any Elephant dung and just for fun, Scotty had installed a system where the swan could, on demand, deposit onto the road 'whitewash' paint from a valve positioned at the rear of the car... all to make the swan car more lifelike!

As you can imagine panic and chaos ensued wherever Scotty and the swan car went. This was of course the intention!

It seems Scotty outdid them all and his car of choice wasn't even a Rolls Royce! The donor vehicle was a Brooke 25/30 from the English firm of car and boat builders JW Brooke!

The machine was later sold to the Maharaja of Nabha and it remained in his family for 70 years. Today, the swan car is owned by the Louwman Museum in The Netherlands

The Swan Car

Rolls-Royce upsets the Maharajah of Alwar!

There's a great story from 1920, when on one of his regular visits to London, the Maharajah of Alwar, Jai Singh was taking a stroll around Mayfair, when he decided to pop into the Rolls-Royce dealer and take a look at his favourite motoring brand. Jai Singh already owned several Rolls-Royces, but as any Maharajah knew, you could never own enough! However, being on his own, without his attendants and entourage, he decided to dress in ordinary English clothing, so he could wander around the city incognito. Once in the showroom, the sales staff took one look at him, decided that he didn't look like anyone who could afford a Rolls-Royce, so completely ignored him!

Jai Singh approached a salesman to enquire about the specification of one of the models on the showroom floor. The salesman refused to engage with him, ignored his request for a test drive and rudely showed the King of Alwar the exit!

Infuriated, insulted, and frustrated, on his return to his hotel, Jai Singh instructed his staff to telephone the dealership and make an appointment for the Maharajah of Alwar to visit the showroom.

Soon after, dressed in the finest rich regalia of a king, The Maharajah of Alwar arrived at the Mayfair showroom, positively dripping in money and jewels. The red carpet was literally waiting for his appearance, as were the dealership's employees, who lined the carpet on both sides to pay respects to the king as he walked by. The sales staff swooned over him for two hours whilst he inspected the six cars in great detail on the shop floor. To even the most experienced Rolls-Royce salesman, it came as somewhat of surprise when the Maharajah decided to buy all six cars, there and then and for cash!

Soon after, the collection of cars, which in today's terms would amount to well over a million pounds were delivered to India and as a way of punishing Rolls-Royce for his earlier treatment, Jai Singh gave the order for all six of the vehicles to be handed over to the municipality of the city to be used as rubbish collectors! The cars were fitted with brushes for sweeping the streets and the backs were loaded with all sorts of garbage the city could produce!

News spread quickly and Rolls-Royce were not just humiliated but mortified at the treatment their cars were receiving. Apologies came fast and furious from Rolls-Royce headquarters regarding the treatment from their salesman. Eventually the Maharajah accepted the apology, and the cars were taken out of civic service!

The phrase 'Don't judge a book by its cover' made popular in 1946, and taken from the murder mystery novel 'Murder in the glass room', by Lester Fuller and Edwin Rolfe, comes to mind!

It wasn't just the Maharajahs in India who were blinging up their cars either.

After India gained independence from Britain in 1947, the Maharajahs fortunes began to wane. They may have owned several Rolls-Royces each, but many now didn't have the wealth to maintain them. Many special cars then were simply put away in barns and garages. Reminders of times gone by. Some were sold locally, others exported as many fell into disrepair and eventually disappeared.

Luckily however, the Indians love of all things Rolls-Royce has been kept alive. There are more fans of the marque in India than anywhere else in the world (according to the Rolls-Royce Facebook fan page) and many of the important Maharajah cars have been rediscovered, restored, and repatriated back to India. There, they are cherished by their owners and the public at the many classic car shows around the country.

The Maharajah cars have become part of India's history, culture and even religion. They're important in the extreme to the world of motoring and will never be matched. The first Maharajah Rolls-Royce delivered to India was in 1908 and is called the 'Pearl of the East'. The first Rolls-Royce off the production line after the Second World War was delivered to a Maharajah, and one of the most famous of all the Indian Rolls-Royces, a car built in 1934 for the Maharajah of Rajkot, known as 'The Star of India' (named after a 563 carat Star Sapphire), after being lost from the country for a few decades, is now back home where it belongs, restored to its former glory and owned by the great grandson of the first owner... Finally, as a note of interest, The new class of Maharajahs, the Bollywood stars, love Rolls-Royces as much as any of their ancestors!

Some interesting Rolls-Royce facts

The 'Spirit of Ecstasy' or flying lady mascot is as famous as the name Rolls-Royce. It's instantly recognisable and is a British icon in itself. The company, as we know, was founded in 1906, but the mascot didn't come along until 1911, so for the first five years of production, no Rolls-Royce was supplied, adorned with a car mascot of any type. However, from around 1910 it became fashionable for car owners to add mascots to the top of their radiator's caps, which were always visible at the front end of the car. Not quite blinging them up like the Maharajahs, but it was a way of personalising a vehicle. Models of dogs, pharaohs, fish, eagles, arrows, plus any number of other sculptured models were available, after market, to have fixed to the end of your bonnet.

This to Rolls-Royce was unacceptable. The directors of the firm felt that the owners were affixing, in many cases, highly inappropriate ornaments to their cars. This really didn't help the company continue to build its reputation as the maker of the 'best car in the world' if one of their models was seen carrying the same radiator ornament as a cheap, inferior motor car. They therefore acted very quickly and commissioned a more dignified and graceful mascot.

The specification was that the model chosen must convey the message in its very appearance of 'speed, silence, grace… and the absence of vibration'!

Sculptor, Charles Robinson Sykes was chosen for the task. He'd a couple of years earlier created a car mascot for a private client, Baron John Montagu, which was attached to his personal Roll-Royce. The figure was modelled on Montagu's secretary and secret lover, Miss Eleanor Thornton. Sykes took the design for this, rearranged it slightly and put it to the Rolls-Royce board with the name 'The spirit of speed'.

The company commissioned Sykes to go ahead with the design and it was re-named 'The Spirit of Ecstasy'. From then on, each new Rolls-Royce would carry the figure of Miss Eleanore Thornton, wherever it travelled around the word!

Tragically, Eleanor, died in 1915 when she was sailing to India with Montagu. The ship they were travelling on was torpedoed by a German U-boat whilst crossing the Mediterranean. Montagu survived.

Times move on and in 2002 Rolls-Royce was bought by BMW… from Volkswagen! (who'd owned the company since 1998). The rights to 'The Spirit of Ecstasy' were owned by Volkswagen and they requested forty million dollars from BMW to transfer the ownership and to allow the new owner to continue using the figure of Eleanor Thornton on their cars!

Around sixty-five percent of all Rolls-Royces ever made are still on the roads

The famous 'Blue Bird' land speed record holding car was clocked in 1933 at 272mph. Driven by Sir Malcolm Campbell, the machine was powered by a Rolls-Royce V12 engine.

Rolls-Royce also supplied the engines for the 'Hurricane' and 'Spitfire' fighter planes during World War Two.

The coach lines, or pinstripes you see running down the length of any new Rolls-Royce are all painted by hand. These are added at the final stage of manufacture and there is no room for error. The special paint used, bonds with the surface immediately. If a mistake were to be made, the whole car would need to be re-painted! Generally, only one man (there hasn't yet been a woman) has the job of doing this and he's one of the highest paid workers in the plant!

One of India's most controversial spiritual leaders to have

ever emerged from the country was Bhagwan Rajneesh. Born in British India at the height of the empire in 1931, Rajneesh became infamous in his lifetime as a mystic and sex guru! He preached emotional, spiritual, institutional and sexual liberation... he built a huge commune and organisation in Oregon, America. In fact, it was described as a utopian city. His followers, all dressed in orange, donated almost all of their money and possessions to him and his movement. This led to accusations of him personally living in ostentation and opulence, whilst his thousands of followers lived a life of poverty. He was described as having a narcissistic personality disorder and was deported from the USA, before finally settling again in India (after more than twenty countries refused him entry).

Public opinion has been changing over the years since his death in 1990, and he's now looked upon by many as a figure being ahead of his time, and as important as Gandhi, or even Buddha himself. He's credited with helping to liberate the minds of future generations from the shackles of religiosity and conformism.

Whatever the truth, or your opinion on Bhagwan Rajneesh, he certainly had great taste when it came to cars. He loved Rolls-Royces... so much so, he owned ninety-three of them! Rolls-Royce the firm loved him almost as much. He was one of their best clients and so they happily flew out factory-trained engineers to maintain his fleet when required.

As well as being known as a 'sex guru' Rajneesh became known in America as the 'Rolls-Royce guru'! He was once quoted as saying that riding in a Rolls-Royce was 'A ride in a tranquillity that compares with the peace of Buddha!'

The largest collection of Rolls-Royces

Brunei, a country positioned on the north coast of the island of Borneo in Southeast Asia was once a British protectorate and part of the empire from 1888, until it gained independence in 1984. Economic growth and a highly fortunate and extensive supply of petroleum and natural gas has created immense wealth for the nation. Its population are amongst the richest in the world, being ranked fifth in the world by gross domestic product per capita. In other words, the people of Brunei have a lot of disposable income… and no one in Brunei has more spending power than the reigning monarch, the twenty-ninth Sultan of Brunei. The Sultan is a huge car fan. So much so, it's estimated he has two thousand five hundred of them in his very large garage, including the biggest single collection of Rolls-Royces on the planet… he has around six hundred!

Hong Kong's love of Rolls-Royces

The British empire's last colony loves Rolls-Royces so much, that there are more in Hong Kong per capita than anywhere else in the world.

Meridian line… timing

The Meridian line is the imaginary line that runs from the North Pole to the South Pole and right through the centre of Greenwich in London. It was set in 1884 as Longitude Zero, much to the irritation of the French!

From that date on, every place on earth was measured in terms of its angle east or west of the Greenwich line.

The line divides the eastern and western hemispheres, as the equator divides the northern and the southern hemispheres

This is where we get the term Greenwich Mean Time, or GMT from.

So, from 1884 GMT became the international time standard with every city in the world setting its time by it, either plus or minus GMT. Prior to this, countries, as well as towns (including towns in Britain) would often work on their own time zone. So, with GMT set as the standard, this helped enormously with train time tables, international communications using the new telegraph systems and the efficient expansion of the empire… it's all about timing!

And as far as time goes, Greenwich is the centre of the world!

Queen Victoria

The second longest reigning British monarch in history after Queen Elizabeth II was not only a Queen, but an Empress and of course she ruled over the largest empire the world had ever known. She was a great supporter of imperial expansion and believed passionately and whole heartedly like most people did in the benefits the empire brought to the world. She believed that the continued expansion of the empire was a force for good, not just for Britain, but for humanity of all creeds and kinds. Britain's role it felt at the time was to spread civilisation throughout its colonies. To make the world British… and therefore a better place!

And Britain could claim a moral high ground here too. Since the early part of the 19th century when Britain abolished slavery, the empire became the first in history to do so and not only that, Britain spent much of the 19th century fighting the slave trade, not just morally, but physically throughout the world and at huge cost financially and in British lives. There are of course huge contradictions here, especially when viewed from the 21st century, but you can see how Britain believed in her cultural superiority to expand its ideals, spread its values, colonise and civilise far flung lands faster and more effectively, before any of the other European power had the chance to stamp their own particular style of empire on the world. It was a race to the top of the empire pile and Britain won.

You can see then how British imperialists, industrialists, entrepreneurs, adventurers, chancers, opportunists, missionaries and philanthropists left Britain's shores positively bulging with the confidence that whatever they decided to do was for the betterment of the empire, the world order and society in general.

There is no doubt about it, it was a strong belief that the British system of governance, law, order and democracy was the best the world had to offer.

Queen Victoria, the person right at the top of that pile, the figurehead of the empire truly believed in that British system of governance. Yet, surprisingly as a woman she was legally powerless to vote in any British political elections... she wouldn't even be able to cast her vote at the local parish council!

However, this didn't concern her one bit and even more surprisingly, Queen Victoria was no fan of the Suffragette movement! In fact, the Queen positively discouraged women to call for 'women's rights' She felt very strongly about this and was unashamedly vocal about it. Queen Victoria felt that a woman's place was in the home, that politics and business were best left to men and that women who fought for the right to vote were unchristian and unnatural for doing so! A woman the Queen said "was a helpmate for a man, but with totally different duties and vocations" This by the way was not an unusual attitude at the time. Many millions of women felt the same, they had no sympathy for the suffrage movement and equally at the same time many millions of men supported the suffragettes! History is never simple or straightforward, it's layered with conflicting facts and even though facts like these can seem shocking or hard to understand to the modern reader, you must remember that times were different then... you can't judge history based on your own thoughts and expectations of life today!

Victoria, whose first name was actually Alexandrina (she just preferred Victoria, which was her middle name) was generally a much-loved queen. She had roads, cities, waterfalls, lakes, schools, buildings and parks named after her and all over the empire (most names have remained to this day)

The public by and large supported, accepted, respected and praised her for her devotion to the job. A job she had no choice over and one that was placed upon her at the age of eighteen. However, no monarch can please all the people all of the time. In her almost 64 years as Queen and Empress, there were eight assassination attempts on her life!

As you can imagine, she was probably not very amused by this, but none of the attempts really fazed her. She once said "It is worth being shot at to see how much one is loved" The British have always loved an underdog and every time someone tried to kill the Queen, her popularity around the empire soured!

She even had her fair share of stalkers. On one occasion a stalker broke into her private quarters, sat on her throne and stole her underwear before making off into the night.

You can thank Queen Victoria for your white wedding dress!

It was the Queen who started the tradition of the bride wearing all white (with no one else allowed to do so!)

In 1840, when Victoria married her cousin, Albert, she wore a long flowing white gown. She was the only one on the day wearing such an outfit because instructions were given that under no circumstances could anyone else wear anything similar to her outfit or indeed any form of white dress! Before that most brides wore their Sunday best on their big day, but soon after Queen Victoria's wedding, brides up and down Britain and then soon around the empire insisted on having a 'white wedding'…Victoria style!

The Queen was quite a linguist. Speaking English and German

fluently with a good grasp of Italian, French and Latin. Her mother and governess were both from German extraction and so Victoria spoke mainly German for the first three years of her life. This developed an unfortunate slight German accent which was in later years dealt through elocution lessons! But the Queens fluent German helped no end in her marriage to her German cousin Albert — servants reported hearing them regularly shouting and arguing with one another… in German!

The European connection to the Royal household shouldn't come as any surprise. All Royal families around Europe were connected through blood then as they are now. Arranged marriages meant that no royal was ever truly 100% native from the country they reigned over! In fact, all current reigning monarchs in Europe today are related. Every one of them can trace their ancestor through the line of King George II of Great Britain… who was in fact a German!

Even though the Queen held the title 'Empress of India' she never did visit that vast country. The long sea journey was thought to be too risky to her health, but she longed to see the exotic land and so she sent painters there to bring back depictions of the places and the people. In the last fourteen years of her life, she even leant Urdu. Taught to her by her 'Munshi' (teacher) and Indian secretary Abdul Karim. It was Abdul who introduce the Queen to curries which she loved. So much so, each day in the royal kitchens, curries we're cooked for lunch!

The discovery of Cocaine

Strictly speaking of course, cocaine had been around for thousands of years. It had been used by indigenous peoples for medicinal, religious and yes, recreational purposes, for generations before the Victorian empire builders discovered and began experimenting with it.

When cocaine arrived in the west, it was celebrated as a modern 19th century wonder drug. Some doctors even suggested that it was literally sent from heaven, from God himself to help cure all sorts of modern-day ailments, such as depression, anxiety, fatigue and migraines... it was also a fabulous cure; it was discovered for alcoholism! The fact it just swapped one problem for another much greater problem, took a while for people to work out!

Sigmund Freud, the founder of Psychoanalysis, that practise of studying the unconscious mind and human behaviour had a particular interest in cocaine! The drug, he truly believed, was indeed the cure for just about anything you can imagine, and it certainly was, he thought, the answer to the social scourge of being addicted to alcohol.

Alcoholism was a serious problem throughout the period. With industrialisation demanding and requiring workers to turn up at their places of work literally on the stroke of a clock, at a certain time, on the dot and then to be there for at least eight hours solid, it was necessary to make sure that the workers were not drunk!

Drinking excessively was quite normal and this was relatively fine if you were working on a farm, feeding cattle, or planting crops out in the countryside. Being slightly drunk most of the day there, was actually doable, and people had been doing it quite well for generations.

However, as these workers migrated from the provinces and into the newly bulging towns and cities and found work in a 19th century industrially revolutionised factory, they really, for safety and productivity reasons, needed to change their drinking habits. In these places, with heavy machinery, highly dangerous conditions and more importantly to the owners, orders to make on time and to a certain standard, being slightly drunk was not acceptable at all… cocaine then, it was hoped, might be the answer to cure drunkenness!

One favourite cure for attempting to get people to stop drinking before the use of cocaine, was to make them suck on an orange for a few hours a day… this, as you can imagine had little effect and it's not known whether many people actually stuck with the programme!

Freud called cocaine a "magical drug" with magical powers, and he wasn't a man to simply talk the talk either. He actually got on with proper human cocaine experiments. First of all, on a scientist friend who was addicted to all sorts of pain relief, including morphine and alcohol. This was all in an attempt to alleviate the misery he suffered daily from a wound that refused to heal. He'd cut his thumb with a dirty scalpel during an experimental autopsy on a cadaver some years earlier, and the injury had been spreading disease and infections ever since.

Freud was quoted as saying that cocaine was effective in curing morphine and alcohol abuse. He was right, especially when it came to his friend… the cocaine he prescribed for him was a real blessing. It certainly helped cure his old addictions. The downside though was that Freud's friend soon became addicted to the rather effective white powder!

Freud liked cocaine a lot — some say, too much! So much was his fascination with it, it's said that he was a user and abuser himself for at least twelve years — all in the course of his experiments!

He prescribed cocaine to other friends too and for all sorts of ailments. It was seen by him as a panacea for just about everything... Freud even sent a gift of cocaine to his girlfriend and told a colleague that it would "make her strong and give her cheeks some colour!" Such a fan of cocaine was Freud, that his first major scientific publication was on the subject... it was titled 'Uber Coca'!

In Britain and around her empire, cocaine was available over the counter. It was sold as a pick-me-up, hang-over cure, it was popped in drinks and was even found in throat lozenges. Cocaine, unlike many 19th-century mad cap concoctions, sold by the so called 'snake oil salesmen' of the day, definitely worked... it did exactly what was expected and, by goodness, it didn't half energise people!

But, what about the snake oil salesman? Before I get back to cocaine, let me tell you about the origins of 'snake oil' and it's not-so-trustworthy salesman! It's a term that although originated in America, was something used all around the world and across the empire to describe the huge amount of strange, often useless and sometimes downright dangerous concoctions made up by dodgy chemists, back-room chancers and even dodgier doctors. Creams, oils, drinks, and pills were peddled by these super slick characters who made a living by travelling around and selling their 'cure all' treatments out of the back of a horse drawn wagon... before, they often had to make a run for it!

The colonies were particularly attractive to the snake oil salesman, because, in the colonies, there was a helpful number of tropical diseases the colonials were petrified of catching and even dying of... Where better then, to sell a 'guaranteed' cure for malaria, dysentery, smallpox and even the Black Death, than in some far flung, sweltering corner of the British Empire!

So, as we know, the term 'snake oil' and its salesman conjure up something on the seedy side of life, and a product certainly not to put any faith in. However, the origins of 'snake oil' couldn't be further from the truth.

During the 19th century, with the American expansion of the railways, in particular the Transcontinental Railroad, tens of thousands of Chinese manual workers were shipped in to carry out the hard labour in unbelievably terrible conditions (very little health a safety about in those days). They worked very long shifts, in all weathers and sometimes under threat from local Indian tribes, who were not happy one bit with the railway line going through their territory. It was a tough life for sure, especially physically, but the workers gained some relief after a long hard shift by rubbing onto their sore bodies, some of their special 'snake oil'. This was an ancient treatment they'd brought with them from their villages and provinces, back home in China. The oil was genuinely made from a snake. The Chinese water snake. This was a snake that was rich in Omega 3 and the Chinese had used its oil for thousands of years in their medicines. When the oil was rubbed into aching muscles, old injuries and tired limbs, the water snake oil had a wonderful effect. It helped alleviate the pain and reduced the swelling, not just from over-worked muscles, but it also cured arthritis pain and other complaints brought on by time, injury or tiredness. It was a much-needed treatment after hours of back-breaking graft.

The Chinese workers shared their exotic ointment treatment with fellow American labourers and the Americans were blown away by its genuine and much-appreciated results. The Americans marvelled at the health giving and health healing properties of the Chinese snake oil. Even those highly sceptical about any benefits that could be gained by rubbing some greasy substance out of an old jar onto aching limbs, were truly convinced once they tried it. No one really knew how or why the Chinese snake oil worked, but no one really cared either. Snake oil was a magic potion, and soon enough the stuff was being heralded as a wonder product. News spread and everyone wanted some. So, up to this point, the Chinese 'snake oil' had a faultless reputation as a genuine product with miracle powers.

But, as we know, as soon as something becomes popular, fashionable, in much demand and in short supply, there will always be people jumping into the market with their own copycat versions to take a piece of the lucrative pie. That's simply capitalism. However, some of these people, especially during the late 19th century, were of dubious character to say the least! They were there to exploit people's hopes, fears and pains, and to profit hugely from selling them their own brand of 'snake oil'. Their oils, along of course with their promises of health-giving results, were usually completely rubbish and of no benefit whatsoever... not much changes!

'Snake oil salesmen' began appearing all over the states and across the colonies flogging magical ointments that bore no resemblance to the original Chinese water snake oil (including the fact that none of them actually worked)! They promised to cure any disease or disorder you had, thought you had, or were worried about catching!

Snake oil then quickly gained a reputation as being a bit on the dodgy side. It still didn't stop people buying into the new versions of it though... there were always plenty of punters willing to believe anything!

There is one particular character who is credited with finally ruining forever the reputation of the original 'snake oil' and this was an entrepreneur and ex cowboy, called Clark Stanley. Stanley jumped in to cash in on the wonders of snake oil and he began marketing and promoting himself as a 'snake oil' expert, with a catchy title he gave himself too… he was known as the one and only 'Rattlesnake King'!

He claimed that he'd learned the secrets of snake oil capture, manufacture and treatments from indigenous American Indian medicine men, and apparently their snake oil was as good as any of the Chinese versions. Interestingly, the native Indians didn't have a history of making snake oil treatments like the Chinese, but that didn't matter… no one knew that!

Not only was this the case, but the rattlesnake oil was nothing in comparison to the Chinese water snake version anyway, especially when it came to its healing qualities. The rattlesnake was particularly short on the natural acids that the Chinese water snake had, including the important Omega 3. The water snake was positively packed with Omega 3 (which is one of the reasons why it was so successful). The fact was that nothing in the oil of the rattlesnake was particularly beneficial to humans… not that this stopped Stanley's marketing campaign claiming the contrary!

Clark Stanley placed advertisements in newspapers across America, promoting his own brand of snake oil. Remember, he was known as 'The Rattlesnake King' so he wasn't the kind of guy who would just sell out of the back of a wagon. No, he was posting his snake oil mail order throughout the land! Stanley even exhibited at trade fairs. Once, at the 1893 World's Fair in Chicago, he demonstrated how his company removed the precious oils from the rattlesnake in front of a live and mesmerised audience. The old cowboy reached into a bag and pulled out an unfortunate, fat rattlesnake. He then quickly and expertly sliced it up and dropped its parts into an already prepared pan of boiling water. He let it bubble a bit as he preached to his audience on the benefits of rattlesnake oil. And, as the snake fat broke away and rose to the surface in the bubbling pan, he carefully skimmed it off with a spatula and placed the precious gunge on a table... not a pretty sight. This, he said to the aghast audience, was the vital ingredient in his snake oil and it was guaranteed to help and heal almost all ailments. His product was called 'Clark Stanley's Snake Oil Liniment' and he had hundreds of pots for sale at the exhibition... the crowds lapped it up and he sold his pots of snake oil like hot cakes!

But, as well as the slight issue of the rattlesnake not having the naturally occurring and required ingredients of the Chinese water snake, there was another, even bigger problem with Stanley's snake oil liniment mixture... it was discovered in 1917 by some federal investigators, who were looking into claims of dodgy practises that Stanley had been accused of, that Stanley's snake oil was not quite what he said it was. The investigators seized one of Stanley's snake oil shipments and tested its ingredients. They were somewhat surprised to discover that his special snake oil, didn't contain any snake oil whatsoever... neither water snake nor rattlesnake! It was found that 'The Rattlesnake King' Clark Stanley's product contained mainly mineral oil, possibly a bit of beef fat, definitely a little red pepper... and a good dose of turpentine spirit!

'The Rattlesnake Kings' credibility collapsed overnight,

as did his product, and Stanley was seriously reprimanded by the authorities for misleading thousands of customers. He was prosecuted for violating the food and drug act and for falsely and fraudulently representing his oil as a remedy for pain and other ailments... for all of this, he was fined just $20! ($500 in today's terms.)

The tiny fine begs the question. Did Stanley offer an official or two something even more desirable than 'snake oil' to get off so lightly... that something known as good old hard cash?

So, poor old 'snake oil', that original Chinese ancient recipe from the exotic east, has forever since been associated with dodgy products, dodgier people and unreliable promises... the exact opposite of its true origins!

But back to cocaine

Before the harmful and addictive consequences were fully understood, cocaine was truly celebrated around the world as a revolutionary medical breakthrough. It was also a fabulous anaesthetic... it completely comatosed people! Actually, compared to what doctors had been using up until this point, cocaine was much safer to use when anaesthetising patients during surgery. Prior to this, chloroform was the method they had for putting people under, ready for an operation. Chloroform certainly worked well, however, sometimes too well! The downside with chloroform, was its horrible reputation for sending people off to sleep forever... every day, patients died not because of a medical mishap, but because of an accidental overdose of chloroform! Cocaine was far more effective and easier for doctors to manage.

Doctors swooned over the qualities and convenience of

cocaine and, in 1885, the highly respected (it still is) British Medical Journal published over sixty articles on the benefits of cocaine. The world fell in love with the stuff!

Cocaine became so normal in modern culture that it even began appearing in novels. Arthur Conan Doyle's magnificently popular series of stories about the hero detective Sherlock Holmes often had the super sleuth, ceremonially, taking out his hypodermic syringe from its fine Morocco leather case and injecting himself with a good dose of cocaine. This seemed to give him the extra brain power and concentration skills required to crack the toughest of cases! Contemporary reviewers of the books loved the Sherlock character and celebrated his antics, including that of taking cocaine on a regular basis!

Readers loved the fact too, that when Holmes was confronted with a particularly taxing case, he could go days without ever sleeping. He was a criminological superman and his superpowers were enhanced with cocaine. Sherlock Holmes was a modern man, living in the capital city of the British Empire, so why wouldn't he be a user of the most modern of all wonder drugs?

So, this wonder drug that could cure everything from seasickness to hay fever was manufactured in all sorts of products, including cocaine sprays, which were used by anyone suffering from a common cold. The cocaine soon took your mind off a blocked-up nose!

And talking of noses, cosmetic surgery really benefited from cocaine too (I'll get to cosmetic surgery a little later) the new drugs anaesthetic qualities were a real boon to the industry with cosmetic surgeons offering to re-sculpt any nose, painlessly, using a shot of cocaine to take away the discomfort and the stress of the operation!

The most fashionable nose shape at the time was that of the classical Roman… the aquiline hook. But, if you weren't born lucky, with that shape of nose, you were unlikely to want to go through the pain, suffering and possible death from chloroform and go under the knife at some doctor's surgery to have a re-shape. Of course, some did anyway, but now with cocaine on the market, cosmetic surgery boomed. Everybody wanted a hooked nose and now, with cocaine, you could, if you had the money, get yourself a proper eagle-like hooter… all without any agony, torture or possible death!

I've mentioned tattoos already and London's famous artist Sutherland Macdonald. Well, he loved cocaine as well. He helpfully used it to inject some of his clients when he was working on a particularly intricate and detailed tattoo. One that might have needed a long period of time to complete. The cocaine would take away the pain of the tattooing and help the time pass pleasantly!

The best-known cocaine-containing product of the period of course is famously, Coca-Cola. Invented in 1885 by John Pemberton, a pharmacist from Atlanta, Georgia, the drink also contained caffeine, so as a stimulant it was far more effective than any 'energy drink' you can buy today!

The drink was advertised as a medicine to cure headaches, upset stomach and fatigue. All of this was probably true and, as a medicine, it proved popular, but because it tasted so good people soon forgot the medicinal reasons for buying it and the drink became known as one of the most popular beverages in the world. The ingredients of Coca-Cola are, as we know, a top secret. We do know however that sometime later, in the early 1900s, all traces of cocaine were removed!

Around the same time, during the early 20th century, it became apparent that cocaine, as well as being beneficial in medicine, was also having some devastating effects on the social fabric of society. Drug addiction and abuse became common. It was proven that violence and criminality were being fed by the use of cocaine. It was discovered that the powder was so addictive that users were turning to anything illegal and lucrative to fund their needs, and the situation looked like it was soon to be out of control... it was far worse than the old problem of alcoholism. There was an increasing fear in governments and the wider public, that drug-fuelled violent criminals we're going to roam and take over the streets of the growing inner cities. Therefore, to nip the problem in the bud, the governments in America, Britain and around Europe, decided to ban the use of cocaine. It, overnight became an illegal drug... I think you'll agree, that seemed to solve the western cocaine problem!

Cosmetic surgery

Cosmetic surgery, or sometimes called 'Plastic Surgery' is actually nothing new. The Greeks were at it 2500 years ago and in fact the word 'plastic' doesn't come from the material surgeons insert into your body to re-shape it. No, it has nothing to do with modern plastics, the word comes from the Greek 'Plastikos' meaning to 'mould' or to 'give shape'

But during the time of the British Empire, with the industrial revolution in full swing and a burgeoning middle class with disposable income, cosmetic surgery really began to take off.

The surgeons at the time were known as 'Beauty Doctors' but unfortunately for many patients, the beauty doctors were often no better than the snake-oil salesmen! Selling dreams, hopes and promises of everlasting youth to unsuspecting, yet very willing clients in the form of dreadful operations (luckily though under the newly discovered anaesthetic or even better Cocaine!) Cream, ointments and powders to rub all over themselves were also invented, which if they were lucky did no harm, but if they were unlucky, maimed them for life! The doctors, many of whom were not medically trained came up with all sorts of new dastardly beauty treatments on a daily basis.

Popular amongst these were scaffolding contraptions cleverly attached to the head of the patient and made from steel rods, nuts and bolts. Twine was then wrapped around pulleys and around the face and under the chin. The twine would be tightened regularly and over a period of time to pull the patients face upwards (a face lift) or tugged in an almost choke hold under their chin to tuck away any unfortunate double chin!

This procedure was remarkably effective whilst the patient was wearing the scaffolding, but once it was removed, everything unfortunately dropped south again… but not until the 'Beauty Doctor' had been paid!

Nose jobs though as I mentioned earlier were quite successful. One of the reasons for this was the ancient medical texts discovered in India by the British in the later part of the 18th century. In these centuries old Indian books, descriptions, methods and even diagram drawings came to light. These showed how surgeons from a forgotten bygone age were operating on, skin grafting and rebuilding noses generations before the British arrived on the continent.

You see, in ancient India there was a genuine demand for such nose operations — noses were often forcibly removed as a punishment for breaking any number of laws. From theft to adultery. And if you were the unfortunate recipient of a tough sentence handed down by a local court… then your nose could very well be cut off! This was a public sign of shame to carry around with you for the rest of your life (if you survived the initially chopping off that is) So, for the rest of your days, your job and love prospects would be seriously and detrimentally effected. However, if you had the money to pay a surgeon at the time, then they could quite possibly solve your problems with a rebuilt nose, cleverly skin grafted onto your face. The medical instructions in the ancient manuscripts included top tips on where to take the skin for the grafting, as well as techniques for the re-moulding of the nose.

So, you can see how and why the ancient Indian cultures developed these skills. As times changed and nose removals became a less popular form of punishment, the skills required to fix the problem faded into the mists of time and they were forgotten … until they were rediscovered by the British.

Like all great empires before them The British Empire took ideas from earlier civilisations, improved them and made them their own… that's how new empires learn and grow!

So, the methods were copied and improved upon and nose jobs became, towards the end of the 19th century a not uncommon procedure.

Another popular request then as now was for the removal of wrinkles on the face, or at least some sort of improvement. Botox and fillers are readily available on the high street today to do that job, but those whom lived at the height of the empire didn't have these wonder products available to them.

Paraffin is great for lamps, or rather it was back then, but the beauty seekers of the empire quite liked it injected into their face to remove wrinkles. They liked it because the beauty doctor told them it worked!

Injecting paraffin was a panacea when it came to wrinkles, they were promised. And so, it was injected liberally into the folds of the skin to fill and smooth natures cruel lines. Unfortunately, most people discovered with the over use of paraffin injections that the liquid had a habit of migrating to other areas of the body, especially if the patient lived in the warmer climes, the tropics of the empire, underneath that sun that never sets. For these unfortunates, they could easily suffer facial disfigurements, which to remedy, they'd be advised to go back for more paraffin injections!

The Empire's love of Curry — The first Indian restaurant in Britain

Most people seem to think that Indian restaurants began appearing in Britain during the 1960/70s. It's true that there was an explosion of new Indian restaurants appearing in most towns during this period, but the British fell in love with curry a long time before this.

The first Indian restaurant in Britain was opened in London in 1810. Fabulously named 'The Hindoostane Dinner and Hooka Smoking Club'. It was located in Marylebone and the target clientele were ex Indian colonials and employees of The East India Company, and of course the wealthy 'Nabobs'. All of whom, in one way or another missed their time living in India. This was as close as they could get to the old days whilst living in London.

The location was ideal for his market, as this was a part of London popular with these colonial returnees, who naturally congregated together socially.

The owner of the establishment was a charismatic and well-liked Bengali called Sake Dean Mahomed. Sake was an entrepreneur, an adventurer, a surgeon, a captain in the British East India Company, a writer and now in 1810, after marrying an Irish girl, living in Cork for twenty years, remarrying and moving to London, Sake became a restauranteur!

The 'Hindoostane' advertised in the local papers that it was a place fitted out in the eastern style, so not only could his customers taste the foods they missed from India, but imagine, in Marylebone, that they were back in the tropics!

Sake also offered a home delivery service, so as well as being the first Indian restaurant in Britain, the 'Hindoostane' was also the very first Indian take-away!

Sake, being a true entrepreneur saw that there was a market for Indian food, but he was probably too soon into the Indian restaurant scene. There wasn't the same culture back then like there is today of 'eating out', and many of his potential customers, although no doubt they tried his restaurant, were wealthy enough to have cooks at home. These cooks were often, originally from India and they could of course cook authentic Indian dishes for their masters, which satisfied their love of eastern-inspired food. And all without having to leave their house or going to the trouble of ordering it to be delivered.

Socialising for the 'Nabobs' and old colonials in London at this time, was more likely to be done in each other's homes, with Indian-inspired dinner parties, as opposed to meeting up in restaurants.

So, despite rave reviews, the running costs of the restaurant were so great that Sake was forced to sell the business around a year after opening it. The restaurant continued for another twenty years under different management, but unfortunately Sake himself went bankrupt soon after selling it.

Never one to be kept down for long though, Sake, soon bounced back, and to keep himself out of debtors' prison, he was offering his services as a butler and a valet. But things quickly improved and he moved to Brighton, where he set up a new business 'Mahmoud's Baths'.

Sake, yet again, was there at the very beginning of something brand new, and this time his timing was perfect. This was the very early days of aromatherapy and with Brighton being the hippest town outside of London, this is where it all started. Water treatments of all types were being offered around the town, but Sake offered something a little more exotic. His treatments were inspired by the tropics and by that land, far away, that most people had never visited and were unlikely to either. Mahmoud's Baths were a little taste of the romance of India… in the heart of Brighton. With his steam rooms and baths all infused with heated aromatic vapours, using Indian herbs and oils, his body massages could cure all sorts of ailments. News spread and the rich and famous flocked to see him.

His business boomed. Before long, he became the 'shampooing surgeon' to King George IV and later William IV. Shampooing in those days referred to an all over body scrub, as opposed to just the hair. So, Sake, the first person to set up an Indian restaurant in Britain had now gained himself a distinguished place within British society, and was mixing with royalty and enjoying the high life on the south coast. He charmed all he met, and he became known and celebrated as 'Dr Brighton!'

The oldest Indian Restaurant in Britain... plus why we drink lager with our Chicken Tikka Masalas!

The oldest Indian restaurant title goes to 'Veeraswamy' located on Regent Street in London. Opened in 1926 by a retired Indian Army officer, Edward Palmer. Palmer was the grandson of an Indian Princess and an English general in the British Army.

He set up an Indian food business in London in 1896 and gave it the name Edward Palmer Veeraswamy & Co. The Veeraswamy in the title, taken from his grandmother, who's name it was before she married his grandfather.

Palmer was known as an expert in Indian cuisine. He had considerable knowledge and was highly regarded in food circles. He even lectured on the subject and wrote on the topic too. He was certainly passionate about it and his successful business imported and sold all sorts of Indian foods, spices and delicacies, with the promise that all E.P. Veeraswamy & Co products could be 'used under Western conditions and yet produce Eastern delights'... The 'Nabobs' loved him!

In 1924, Palmer was called upon to offer advice on setting up an Indian restaurant within the Indian Government Pavilion at the British Empire Exhibition of that year. Who better than the leading expert in London on Indian food to advise the government on setting up a restaurant to promote India at the exhibition?

Palmers' expertise and advice paid off. The official Indian Government report after the event showed that the Indian restaurant was a roaring success. Huge crowds were pulled in to taste a little of the eastern exotic foods on offer and the British public fell head over heels in love with the flavours, the excitement and the atmosphere of the surroundings created by Palmer. So genuine were the dishes that Indian visitors also enjoyed visiting the restaurant and over five hundred curries were served daily throughout the show.

The following year in 1925, Palmer was not only the food advisor at the Empire Exhibition, but his company was called in by the Indian Government to run the whole restaurant itself. So, the company E.P Veeraswamy diversified from importers and wholesalers of Indian foods, into proper, fully functioning restauranteurs. The restaurant could seat two hundred people and again, the enterprise was a victory, with thousands of curries served and the public desperately wanting more of the same after the exhibition closed.

The two British Empire Exhibitions of 1924 and 1925 were the best market research any company could ever wish for. It was now obvious which route the firm was going to take, so in 1926 Veeraswamy Indian Restaurant was opened on Regent Street, London.

The restaurant is still there today, as famous as it ever was. It's changed hands several times, but now boasts a Michelin star and it can lay claim to introducing the ritual of drinking cold lager with your Indian meal!

Prince Axel of Denmark was a big fan of Veeraswamy's and on one visit to the restaurant, he brought with him a cold barrel of his favourite Carlsberg lager to wash the delicious food down with. Then, following that, as a gift, the prince began sending a barrel of the drink to the restaurant each year, and so the restaurant began serving Carlsberg to its clientele (everybody wanted to try the drink of Prince's with their exotic food)! Carlsberg proved to be so popular with Indian food lovers, that Veeraswamy's began importing it to enable them to have a good constant supply for their demanding thirsty customers, who loved lager as much as the food!

Other Indian restaurants began opening up and the tradition of serving ice cold lager with your Indian dish was born.

You can thank the British Empire for all the above!

Eccentrics and parachutes. Not the best mix!

In 1837, parachuting was still in its infancy. People had been jumping out of trees, whilst holding pieces of fabric above their heads for hundreds of years, and with varying degrees of success, but the first public recorded jump from any substantial height was in 1783. The jumper holding on to what looked like a parasol leapt off the top of a building and from around fifty feet. The daredevil survived and was heralded as a bit of a hero, as well as a bit of a loony! But the earliest form of a recognizable parachute jump was in 1785 in France when Jean-Pierre Blanchard demonstrated publicly a safe parachute decent from a hot air balloon, several hundred feet in the air. He bravely strapped his dog to the chute and threw him overboard! Luckily, the experiment was a great success and the dog survived. Jean-Pierre later claimed that he also had made a similar jump... although no one witnessed that one!

With any form of flight being in its very early stages, in those days, people were more occupied with coming up with ways of staying in the air safely, not jumping out of it. So, as a sport, parachuting didn't really capture the imagination. It was purely a novelty performed by the exceptionally daring... or of course, dogs!

But in 1837, an English watercolour artist and eccentric by the name of Robert Cocking appeared on the scene. He was sixty-one years old, and he'd had no personal parachuting experience whatsoever. This didn't stop him from being fascinated with it though and for a couple of years previously, he'd been coming up with new shapes and designs for parachutes. Being an artist, he was pretty good at drawing the designs too and they looked quite good on paper. He was convinced, after carrying out tireless scientific type calculations, based on his parachute shape, height and weight, that his design was a winner, and it would change parachuting forever.

Once he felt confident that all was ready, Cocking had his parachute manufactured and then he approached a couple of chaps he knew who owned a hot air balloon. These were the owners of a very famous machine indeed. The air balloon named the Royal Nassau. He asked them if they'd help him test out his parachute design. This would mean taking him and his contraption two miles up in the air and dropping him and his parachute from that height. Despite knowing that Cocking was not a scientist, or had any experience in parachuting, or indeed making parachutes, the balloon owners agreed!

News soon spread about the upcoming dangerous experiment and the public became very excited indeed. So much fuss was being made over the event, that it was decided to make the jump the main attraction at the Grand Day Fete in Vauxhall, south London in July of 1837.

Posters advertised the demonstration as an 'Extraordinary Novelty and Combined Attraction'. The combined attraction was first of all, the ascent to a great height of the famous Royal Nassau balloon. The balloon would also transport the newly invented parachute with it. This would be followed by the second and most dramatic of the attractions – the inaugural decent of Mr. Cocking in his newly-invented parachute… dropped from two miles up!

Other entertainment was put on by bands, an orchestra and a play or two, but the crowds amassed and paid their entrance fee to watch the aeronauts compete these two amazing death-defying feats!

With thousands in attendance, Mr. Cocking's design was strapped to the underside of the hot air balloon. The parachute consisted of a cone shaped chute, which was a massive 107 feet in circumference. Attached to the chute by cables was a wicker basket... this is where Robert Cocking sat.

At 7.35pm the great balloon took off, carrying with it, hanging below, Mr. Cocking in his basket and fixed to his parachute.

The plan was to take the contraption up to eight thousand feet (just over 2.4 miles). At this point, the two pilots in the balloon would release Mr. Cocking in his basket, so he could float down to his adoring audience. However, it was discovered once they eventually reached five thousand feet, that a miscalculation had been made. The combined weight of the three men, the balloon and the parachute was too great to be able to reach the desired eight thousand feet within the hours of daylight. If they continued at the current rate of accent, taking into account the miscalculated weight, the parachute decent would not take place until late in the evening. Meaning the drop would be in the dark. The crowds below had been waiting long enough for them to get to five thousand feet. If they had to wait much longer, they'd begin to get agitated, and they wouldn't be happy at all. Especially if the big demonstration of modern technology, and of course of daring, couldn't even be seen because it was pitch black at night!

Therefore, after a discussion shouted between the two balloon pilots and Mr. Cocking, it was agreed that they would release the parachute, before it got too late and dark.

Therefore, the chute and Mr. Cocking were released at five thousand feet, and for the first few seconds, although the decent seemed more rapid than anyone was expecting, all looked to be going to plan. However, due to the miscalculations with the weight as mentioned earlier, plus, it was immediately discovered the flimsy construction of the apparatus and the weak stitching in the fabric, the decent gained substantial and unexpected speed… then, within a few more seconds, the parachute suddenly turned completely inside out on itself and the whole, now jumbled up mess of chute, basket, Mr. Cocking and cables began literally dropping like a stone.

Very sadly for Robert Cocking, the demonstration turned out to be about as disastrous as could ever be imagined. The crumpled and broken chute and basket were un-savable and they plummeted downwards towards the ground (luckily, not directly above the shocked crowds, looking upwards).

At around three hundred feet, witnesses saw the basket with Mr. Cocking still clinging on inside, break away from the remains of the canopy and, within seconds, it hit the ground and Robert Cocking was killed instantly.

Mr. Cocking went down in history as the first confirmed parachute fatality, and after this, as you might imagine, parachuting became even less popular with even the bravest of the dare devils, and it was confined to circus and carnival acts, from relatively low heights!

It would take another sixty years or so before developments in the design of parachutes were such, that people began again looking at the potential of ascending safely from great heights whilst being strapped to a flapping canopy of canvas.

Mr Cocking in his parachute, just before being released

First Female Politician

The first woman ever to be elected into the British House of Commons might seem a surprising choice, but it shows how British democracy works. A democratic and 'fair play' system that many countries around the world found exceptionally strange at the time (many still do!)

She was the Irish politician Constance Georgine Markievicz, also known as Countess Markievicz and she was elected in December 1918.

Born Constance Georgine Gore-Booth in London in 1868 (she later married a wealthy Polish landowner)

Constance came from an Anglo-Irish family and her father was the Arctic explorer and adventurer Sir Henry Gore-Booth and the family owned an estate in Ireland.

Prior to being elected on behalf of the Irish nationalist party Sinn Fein, Constance was a well-known socialist, artist, actress, suffragette and revolutionary. In fact, she was prosecuted by the British courts as a revolutionary! You see, she took part in the Easter Rising of 1916, when Irish republicans attempted to force the British out of Ireland and establish an Irish republic. Constance was sentenced to death for her part in the rebellion (including shooting a policeman and a soldier… one of them dead) but this was commuted to life in prison on grounds of her being a woman! When told that she was not going to be executed she responded by saying "I wish you lot had the decency to shoot me"!

She was later released under a government amnesty and although she was elected to the House of Commons in London, Constance never did take up her seat. This was in accordance with Sinn Fein policy, then, as it is now… plus the fact she was serving time in Holloway prison for another offence!

Australia

The name is derived from the Latin *Terra Australis* meaning
    'Southern Land'

You couldn't get much further away from the epicentre of the British empire (London) than Australia. The vast majority of British emigrants to that huge mass of land, a continent in itself never returned to Britain. This would be for all sorts of reasons, but whether the move was successful or not, travelling back to Britain, due to the distance, dangers, time and cost involved was invariably not an easy option. For many people in fact, they knew for certain they'd never return to Britain once they'd left for Australia.

So, the decision to move to Australia was quite a profound one… Especially if you found yourself in court and that decision was made by a judge!

Britain had been sending convicts to Australia since the very first batch were dispatched there on what was called 'The First Fleet' in 1787. America had been the preferred destination for what were seen as 'undesirables' from society, but due to the empire being kicked out as rulers of America in that unfortunate (for Britain) war of independence a few years earlier, the empire needed to find an alternative… and that, thanks to British explorer Captain James Cook was Australia.

The First Fleet was made up of eleven ships, comprising two Royal Navy vessels, six convict ships and three supply ships. 1500 people in total. Of that 1500, around 800 were convicts, from as young as 7 years old and from Britain, Ireland, The West Indies, America and Africa. The rest were government officials, soldiers and pioneer families who were taking a leap of faith to move to the other side of the world in search of a better life.

Today, a direct flight from London to Australia takes around 20 hours non-stop flying. All that time cooped up in an aeroplane might sound horrific to you in your soft 21st century mind set (it does me) but consider this: In 1787 in took the 'First Fleet' eight months to get there. 250 hard days and nights of sailing!

And the conditions were truly horrendous, not just for the convicts either, who spent most of their time locked below in the dark and damp confines of the ships belly (many of whom died en route from typhoid, scurvy, dysentery and fever) but also for the free families, soldiers, crew and civic officers. Their conditions were better, they could at least get some fresh air, they weren't chained together or whipped occasionally, but this was no luxury world cruise!

Every one of the passengers, adult, or child, freeman or convict also knew that there was every possibility they wouldn't even make it to their intended destination (Botany Bay). The chances that the ships might sink were very real (barely anyone could swim. In fact, even Captain James Cook, he who discovered Australia for Britain a few years earlier, couldn't swim!) Fire breaking out mid ocean was a great fear too, as were the ships being separated in a storm. Extreme physical and mental hardship then, non-stop, day and night for

35 weeks. How does that make you feel...? that flight really doesn't sound too bad now does it?

As for the convicts' sentences, these ranged from 7 years to life and could be for low grade and low value crimes like steeling food, poaching and some form of fraud, up to assault and violence. There were also cases of convicts having the wrong political opinions, or thoughts... transporting these people to the other side of the world was an old-fashioned way of 'cancelling' them... just like we do today through social media!

But sometimes, what seems like a terrible live experience can often turn out for the better and this was the case with many Australian convicts. Opportunities arose because it wasn't just a case of locking up prisoners once they arrived in Australia. Convicts were generally put to work utilising any skills they might have while they were incarcerated. Farmers, carpenters, blacksmiths, labourers, all had their usages in a new colony. Skills were picked up along the way too whilst the prisoners, built roads, public buildings, bridges, hospitals and developed farms and prepared the land in the vast areas opening up to the regularly arriving free settlers.

Educated prisoners were used for record keeping, administration and secretarial work. The prisoners helped develop everything required to set up a brand-new British style country half way around the world from the old one!

Once a prisoner had served their time, they were of course released. Some did make it back to Britain, but most decided to stay and work within the free community, amongst their fellow countrymen, the settlers. There was plenty of work on offer too in the ever-expanding settlements, so unemployment wasn't much of an issue. Some prisoners, for good behaviour were even given land grants to build their own homes and farm and both the settlers and the ex-cons generally rubbed along perfectly well together.

Transportation of convicts from Britain and its colonies to Australia lasted for 80 years, ending in 1867. In total 162,000 men, women and children were sent there, mainly for petty crimes and most remained to build their lives once they were free. The total European population of Australia in 1868 once transportation had ended was over 1.5 million. So, the population was from the beginning mainly made up of free settlers, pioneers from the British Isles and Ireland.

Interestingly, the very first form of a police force in Australia called the 'Night Watch' was made up of well-behaved ex-convicts who'd been transported there, had served their time and then given the job of law enforcement on release!

But not all convicts were so compliant on arrival or during their incarceration of sorts in Australia. Even though their prospects once they'd served their sentence were in most cases, ironically far better in Australia than in Britain, the country they'd been forced to leave in shackles and chains, some just couldn't help themselves... they wanted freedom and independence without spending anytime as prisoners!

Here come the 'The Bushrangers'

Bushrangers were escaped convicts who whilst on the run from the authorities roamed the countryside committing crimes and using the vast Australian bush as a refuge. The bush was a place to hide and live out their lives without being locked up, or restricted by the law. They'd periodically make an appearance in public to rob a traveller, a mail coach, a bank or a homestead. They were the Australian equivalent of the British 'Highwayman' or the American 'Outlaw'.

Generally desperate characters, not averse to the odd bit of hostage taking or murder. They were notoriously difficult to track down and over time the Bushrangers developed great bush survival skills and could keep one step ahead of the British authorities, who were under funded and under manned. It wasn't just escaped convicts who took to the bush either. Released prisoners who fancied continuing a life of crime down-under once they'd served their time, would take to the bush, as did many sons of Bushrangers, who joined the family business as soon as they were old enough to fire a rifle.

Australia's best-known bushranger, was Ned Kelly, who shot to fame in the 1870's (literally). Kelly, even today divides opinion in Australia. Some see him as a working-class hero, or a 'Robin Hood' type character (although he wasn't known for giving to the poor!) and others as a violent criminal and murderer to boot.

Ned was the son of a transported convict John Kelly who'd served his 7 years sentence for stealing and selling two pigs and then remained in Australia to build a life for himself. John, didn't take to the bush to be a bushranger, but rather he seemed to have got on with his life, making his way relatively well for a number of years. But, sometime later he was again in prison, this time for possession of stolen goods and soon after being released from prison a second time, John died of 'dropsy'. An incurable condition in the 19th century which causes fluid retention and swelling in the arms and legs. The condition can be brought on for a number of reasons, including liver, heart or kidney problems.

Ned Kelly was 12 when his father died and the eldest male in the household. This left the family without a father and a provider and Ned pointed the finger of blame directly at the authorities, especially the police and he soon took to a life of crime. The first of many arrests came soon after, along with several spells in prison, the longest being for 3 years.

In 1878 things began to get very serious indeed. After a police confrontation at his family home, a shoot-out ensued and Ned was indicted for attempted murder. There was only one thing for it at this point and that was to take to the bush. He'd been associated with 'Bushranger' gangs for some time, but now with a charge of attempted murder hanging over his head, becoming a full-time bushranger, he obvious decided was the only option.

Infuriated that his mother was subsequently arrested and imprisoned for her part in the shootout, Ned vowed to avenge her from the bush. Not long later, Ned, his brother Dan and two others shot dead three policemen… now, murder was the charge, the chase was really on and the public were reading about Ned Kelly and his gang of 'Bushrangers' in newspapers all over the empire.

On the run for two years, Ned went on a crime spree of thefts, raids and murder. All of which were reported in the newspapers including Ned Kelly's manifesto letter in which he denounced the police, the Australian government and rejected the British Empire! Well, the empire felt the same about him. They wanted him rejected and worse!

With Kelly's new found fame, he started demanding justice for the rural poor and of course his family, who he'd felt were all unfairly treated by the police and authorities and he made open threats upon anyone who gave him up to the police, or gave evidence against him… the threats were taken seriously!

All of this news pouring out of the Australian outback was utterly delicious to the press at the time. The newspapers were rolling off the printers at a great rate as people clambered to read about Ned Kelly's most recent adventures and dastardly deeds!

People thought it couldn't get any juicier until they read about Kelly's last stand against the police. In 1880, Kelly and his gang attempted to derail and ambush a police train. With murderous intentions, the gang were dressed in home-made bullet-proof armour (made up from stolen metal ploughs, slung over their chests) The attack was a disaster and in the ensuing gun battle with the police, the whole gang apart from Ned Kelly were killed. Ned was injured, captured, arrested, put on trial and sentence to death by hanging.

Thousands of Ned Kelly supporters marched in rallies, organised petitions and demanded Kelly be released from jail and made a free man. He was innocent they said, a victim of police brutality and they seemed to think he wasn't all that bad really! The crowds also accused the police of arbitrarily arresting, interrogating and holding known associates of Kelly's without any evidence of wrong doing.

In the polices' desperate attempt to find Ned Kelly, this was most certainly true, but the authorities took no notice of the demands, or the allegations. The stories, the twists and the morbid fascination of it all did make great reading though! The public took sides, some openly and secretly admiring Ned Kelly and others siding with the authorities.

Ned Kelly's execution was duly carried out and his last words were famously reported around the world, much to the extreme delight of countless newspapers and their readers.

As the noose was placed around Ned Kelly's head, he said "Such is life"!

The hanging of Ned Kelly was the beginning of the end of the bushrangers. The police and authorities became much better funded and much more able to communicate with one another over large distances through the use of the new telegraph system, which was sprouting up all over Australia and in fact, the rest of the empire. Connecting people in as a dramatic and sudden way in the 19th century, as the internet did in the late 20th century. The telegraph network was good for general communication, good for business, good for the expansion of the empire and great for crime fighting!

Bushrangers, especially Ned Kelly from that time on became cultural icons to some in Australia. Symbols of rebellion against authority, freedom against the empire in their day and representing freedom today for Australia to become a republic with a president as opposed to a constitutional monarchy, with its historical and colonial connections to Britain.

Emigration to Australia from Britain and Ireland boomed in the 19th century, especially after the gold rushes of the 1850's and up until the end of the Second World War. These immigrants made up the vast majority of the population. Since the war though, the demographics have changed with many more people moving from the rest of Europe and Asia.

Today, Australia is one the world's most successful countries with a high standard of living and strong economy. The population is around 26 million, which is the lowest population density of any country on earth. The country is 32 times bigger than Britain and its largest sheep farm is bigger than the whole of Yorkshire (Yorkshire being Britain's biggest county)

The original peoples of Australia, the Aborigines, who'd been there for 50,000 years before colonisation make up around 720,000 of the country's population today. This is estimated to be roughly the same population number that lived there when the 'First Fleet' arrived in 1787.

New Zealand: Australia's quieter cousin has a similar empire history, but without the penal colonies. Named by Dutch explorers' afterthought, Dutch province Zeeland. The country is referred to as 'Aotearoa' by native Māori people... meaning 'Long White Cloud'

The world knows all about New Zealand lamb, but did you know that the first frozen shipment of meat sent to Britain from New Zealand was in 1882? New Zealand in 1893 was also the first country in the world to grant all women the vote... decades before the suffragettes made their mark in Britain... Colonialist, by their very spirit have always been a little quicker off the mark!

Both countries are products of the empire, both are highly successful, have a high standard of living, life expectancy and their constitutions are of course modelled on the British one.

But one of the biggest differences between the countries is this:

Australia is home to more venomous snakes than anywhere in the world... New Zealand has no snakes whatsoever!

The two countries then, the empire can claim as 'jolly good examples' There has always been good humoured rivalry between these two groups of colonials, located down-under, far away from Britain in those feared Southern Ocean's and of course we know of the famous light hearted rivalry between them and Britain itself... in sport, particularly where New Zealand and Australia fair exceptionally well indeed!

But, as much as they relish beating the old country at cricket and rugby, they reluctantly have to acknowledge that it was the old country who invented the games they've become especially good at. The ancient cultural connections, rivalries, history and common bonds remain!

Colonial Accents

The distinctive Australian and New Zealander accents which are actually quite different to one another are absolute products of the British Empire and only exist because of it.

Britain itself has more regional accents per square mile than any other country in the world. County, town and even village to village, the differences are easily distinguished. As an example, there are definite and many variations in the Yorkshire accents and these can change by simply crossing a river from one place to another!

The Scottish accent in the Highlands is markedly different to that in the Lowlands and even though Edinburgh and Glasgow are only 42 miles away from one another, the accents are poles apart. Irish the same, north, south, east and west.

So, when the early settlers from all around Britain moved to those two far off places down-under, they not only took with them their ways of life, culture, ideas and dreams to be transplanted into the new lands, but they also too with them their very different accents!

It was an amazing experiment when you come to think about it. Imagine what would happen today if you put all the British and Irish accents mentioned above, mix in some deep Welsh, a bit of Cockney and a smattering of Cornish and put those accents (people) all in one brand new town to live and work together.

Wait a generation or two and the children of the settlers, born in the new land would come out the other side with accents that sounded remarkably like an Australian or New Zealander today!

This accidental accent development experiment, as a matter of interest was noted in 1820 when the native-born colonists' speech was recognisably different from any accent ever heard in Britain!

Of course the same can be said for the African colonial accents too, but they developed a little differently with influences coming in from the Dutch descended Afrikaners and the many different indigenous African groups. Words themselves, and not just the way words were spoken from both the Afrikaner and African languages also crept into the English spoken there. And just like in Britain, there are great variations. Accents within accents if you like. A colonial Cape Town accent is quite different to a Zimbabwean one.

The same happened in North America and fascinatingly, if you search online for voice recordings of Americans speaking in the late 19th and early 20th century, you'll discover American voices from the past that don't sound much like Americans of today!

From civil war soldiers recounting their exploits to political speeches by President Theodore Roosevelt, you'll discover these colonials sound remarkably British!

The North American accents though, over the years have continued to change and develop with a much more mixed immigration melting pot… so, the empire can't really lay claim to them any more!

Hong Kong — founded on tea and drugs!

Hong Kong as we know it was founded on tea and drugs… I'll get to those juicy facts in a moment!

I mentioned Hong Kong right at the beginning of the book and used its hand over back to the Chinese on 1st July 1997 as a date some say the British Empire, officially gave up the ghost and came to an end.

The date though of the hand over was not something that was thought up in a rush in recent times, as the empire crumbled and shrank, but a date set at the height of the empire, back in 1898. This was when a 99-year lease for the island was agreed upon and signed between the Chinese and the British… but, in truth, if Britain and the empire had maintained world dominance, as they expected, that lease would certainly have been extended. In reality however, the end of the agreement coincided naturally with the end of the empires' power.

But Hong Kong became a colony of the British Empire a little earlier than the date of the 99-year lease. This was in 1841 and so the territory was under the control, management and influence of Britain, it's culture and governance for 156 years. Apart from, that is, an almost four-year Japanese occupation during the Second World War, after the Japanese launched an overwhelming military assault on Hong Kong and defeated the British, Indian, Canadian and local Hong Kong volunteer forces in a fierce 18-day battle. The timing of the attack was astonishing (8 hours after the Japanese bombed Pearl Harbour) and came as a shock to the empire and as a declaration of war on it.

What followed was a period of harsh, petrifying and bloody marshal law, which saw the population of Hong Kong, after a policy of forced migration by the Japanese reduce from 1.6 million to 600,000.

One million residents were transported to parts of mainland China and other places around the region to help reduce, what the Japanese worried, was the risk of the local population supporting an allied re-invasion of Hong Kong. Many of course were used in forced labour camps with tens of thousands executed.

After the end of the World War Two war in 1945, Hong Kong resumed its status as a colony of the British Empire, but was described from then on as 'living on borrowed time' due to the fast-approaching end of the lease with China, and the almost unbearable financial cost of the first and then second world wars. These effectively bankrupted the empire, so any previous hopes of extending the lease with China were scuppered.

Located at the tip of communist China, capitalist Hong Kong continued to thrive in its final decades and throughout the 'cold war' of the 20th century. In fact, its location was crucial during this time and was seen as the 'Berlin of the east' It was not only a hotbed of capitalism, culture and opportunity, but also of espionage, being the centre of British and American anti-communist operations in the Far East.

But back to the fascinating subject of tea and drugs!
Hong Kong was ceded to Britain as part of war reparations paid by China after their defeat in the First Opium War. The conflict lasted from 1839 to 1842 and the first finger of blame for it can be firmly pointed at the British Empires love of tea!

We still do love our tea, but it's not quite the same as it used to be. Or rather it's not viewed in the same way — we just don't appreciate tea like we used too!

When tea was first introduced to Britain in the 17th century, it was colossally expensive. One pot of tea might cost a couple of hundred pounds to make in today's terms. It was for the super-rich only, which is why you'll find on all antique tea caddies, rather nice looking, but intentionally secure locks! Servants were known and expected to steal tea when they could. There was a massive black market for tea, fake tea, dodgy tea and even tea that was very to kill you! I cover the history of tea in my first book 'A Romp With The Georgians' so I won't repeat it here... but it is fascinating!

So, here is why tea is the first culprit when it comes to the Opium Wars with China. Tea in the early days came from China only and China was very happy, for obvious reasons to sell the luxury drink to the Europeans. Britain in particular was a huge buyer. The payment for the tea was in goods (watches, clocks and other western made objects) and silver.

But silver was the commodity China preferred and increasingly insisted upon. This was fine for a while, until the British Government realised a looming, in fact empire threatening problem. They calculated that it wouldn't be too long before China held the majority of silver in the world. This they knew would cause a worldwide economic imbalance, a threat to world stability and the west generally, so something needed to be done.

It was the East India Company (Them again. Remember the India debacle?) who were the main importers of tea to Britain at the time.

In fact, they held the exclusive licence for the importation of tea, issued by the British Government and so, quite cleverly, the price of tea was effectively fixed between the government and the company, keeping it high, which made sure there was plenty of cash to go around! They did have to compete with illegal tea smugglers and the fakers, but generally both the government and the company were controlling a rather profitable 'cash cow' of a trade!

But the silver stock issue was causing problems and to solve it, the British Government insisted that the East India Company come up with an alternative method of payment for the tea, instead of silver.

The Chinese tea merchants were getting more than enough western watches in trade, so they refused any more of those.

However what the Chinese did quite like was opium, and luckily for the East India Company, they had huge areas of land in India where opium grew in abundance.

So, it didn't take a genius intellect to work out a deal between the British and Chinese merchants in which it was agreed that they'd use opium as payment for the tea and not silver. This, for the Chinese dealers was heaven sent. They took payment for the tea in opium, with the opium valued at wholesale price. They then re-sold the opium to their Chinese buyers at retail price, with a massive margin, making much more money than they ever did by taking silver in payment for their tea... a 'double blessing' all round!

This then, all sounds like a fair business arrangement, where everyone wins. The British government keeps its silver, which protects the British economy, The East India Company is without doubt making more profits, as are the Chinese merchants who just can't get enough opium to satisfy the insatiable demand from the Chinese public and the British 'tea tax' still flows nicely back to London!

Why no one thought of this perfect business arrangement before was certainly a question which was asked!

The problem though arose when millions of Chinese people became addicted to the opium which was now awash throughout China. This brought on all the devastation you can imagine with drug overdoses, crime waves and a general break down in civil society.

The Chinese authorities, in an attempt to bring the situation under control, simply decided and decreed to ban opium. They made it illegal. This, they imagined was going to stop the drug coming into the country and wreaking havoc, so that would be the problem solved then?

We know in our modern world that when it comes to drugs, this doesn't work... and it didn't work then either!

When there are incalculable amounts of money to be generated, drug dealers will get around and break any law to maintain that never ending torrent of cash. Officials will be bribed, lip service will be paid, blind eyes will be turned and threats will be made. Remember, it's all about the money... then and now. It's no different.

And this is exactly what happened in the late 1830's. The East India Company and the Chinese Tea Merchants (as well as corrupt Chinese officials) could not and would not stop trading in opium. This was the currency they wanted in payment for their tea. The idea of going back to payment in silver and watches was unthinkable… the profit margins would be slashed and they were just too used to making mountains of money.

So, all involved simply ignored the opium ban, they continued trading as normal, and overnight, they all became illegal drug dealers!

Confrontation then was bound to come. China attempted to clamp down on the trade by impounding western trading vessels, carrying, not just opium, but all sorts of other trade goods. Chinese tea merchants (now drug dealers) were arrested on mass and even British subjects, sailors and merchants were arrested too.

The tea / opium supply chain was being upset and so tea was not flowing back to Britain like it was before (never deprive the British of their tea!) Opium was going to waste, even worse than that, it was being burned by the Chinese authorities. Cash flow then for all concerned was dramatically reduced, and in some cases, cut off.

Add on top of this, the lack of revenue in much needed and expected taxes for the British government on the tea that wasn't being imported and you have a volatile situation to say the least. In fact, these were the ingredients for a violent and perfect 19th century kind of international confrontation!

Britain demanded that China reopen her trade immediately and insisted she sticks to the principles of 'free trade' amongst nations!

As for any British subjects imprisoned. This, the British said was intolerable and insisted they be released unharmed and at once. Along with any British vessels and all British owned merchandise (including opium!)

China refused and even threatened the death penalty for future offenders... Chinese or British.

An insufferable situation, Britain's European competitors (with their own empire ambitions) were watching intently and the British could not stand by, back down and let the Chinese go unpunished. It would be a weakness and their standing in the world would be shattered if they did.

There was only one thing for it... send in the gun boats!

So, the first 'Opium War' started, also called the 'Anglo-Chinese War'. There was another one a little later in the 19th Century. Both conflicts won by Britain, although, the second one with help and an alliance with France... even competitors need to join forces sometimes! But it was after the first war that Britain took Hong Kong as a colony for the empire.

Singapore, another of Britain's Far East territories was founded in 1819 by Sir Stamford Raffles (the famous hotel named after him) as a trading post of the British Empire. It too was occupied by the Japanese during World War II and gained self-governance from Britain in 1959.

Today Hong Kong is the second richest city in the world, after New York (based on the number of billionaires there) and Singapore is the second richest country in the world after Luxembourg (based on gross domestic product per capita)

You've heard of the 'Great British Spirit' well how about some 'Great British Spiritualism'?

During the 19th century, spiritualism became incredibly popular throughout the empire. Although the empire builders were about as modern as you could possibly get. They were inventors, scientists, engineers and leaders in technological advancements, the fascination with spiritualism (some called it ancient witchcraft) and especially with the potential of life after death, swept across the British Empire, Europe and America.

Spiritualism offered something a little different to the kind of 'ever-after' promised by the established church (for good behaviour only) so spiritualism was of great interest to a lot of people!

And so, the practise not only offered the prospect of life after death, but just as interesting, it gave those who practised spiritualism the chance to actually communicate with the dead in the here and now, through seances and mediums.

Queen Victoria can take a lot of the credit for the explosion in spiritualisms popularity. You see, once her beloved husband and consort Prince Albert died at the young age of 42 of Typhoid Fever (a not uncommon disease to catch at the time) the distraught Queen went into her period of official mourning. This was traditional at the time. A widow would be expected to 'mourn' for a period of two years. This consisted of wearing nothing but all black clothing and veils, head to toe.

No bright colours, or anything particularly fashionable either — along with black jewellery made from jet, enamel and dull metals, as well as lockets filled with the deceased hair was the acceptable look of 'mourning'.

Something which was expected of the Queen and Victoria certainly obliged. However, she took the mourning period to an all-time high and new level, never seen before... she wore black and mourned for the rest of her life. This was a period 40 years, right up until her death in 1901.

And with the public seeing the Queen on visits or in the

newspapers wearing a constant range of one form of black clothing or another, this created great interest in that particular colour, especially for the fashion conscious, magazine and lifestyle journal reading middle and upper classes. They adapted the 'mourning' look, but gave it a modern and up to date twist and cut. No longer did you have to be in a state of mourning to wear black. The colour became the height of fashion. Everything became black. Clothes, furniture, carriages (previously they were often painted in bright colours... yellows, reds etc) and just about anything else you can think about became black. From book bindings to black slate fireplaces... plus the clocks that sat on top of them... black, became the new black!

But back to spiritualism

Victoria and Albert were known to have an interest in the super natural and they often took part in seances during the early years of their marriage, so they were very much open to the general ideas of spiritualism.

Soon after Alberts early demise in 1861, the queen was contacted by a young boy who claimed to have a message from beyond the grave — from Prince Albert himself, which would not have been an unexpected surprise to Victoria.

Thirteen-year-old Robert James Lees from Leicester, England was taking part in a family seance session in which he said that Albert had come through from the other side and spoke to him about the queen.

The prince asked for Queen Victoria to be informed that he wished to communicate with her through the medium, the boy Robert James Lees.

Robert had a message for Victoria, direct from Albert and

to prove that it really was the queen's consort communicating from the spirit world, Albert used a pet-name for his wife. One used only by the couple and known only to themselves. Once Queen Victoria was told of this, she sent immediate two of her court members to partake in a seance with the boy.

The prince duly came through during the sitting, he greeted the courtiers by their correct names and gave them accurate information regarding personal details which convinced the queens representatives that the boy medium was genuine and that he really did have direct access to Albert.

Robert Lees was immediately invited to Windsor Castle to conduct seances with the queen in which Albert was called. The spirit of the prince came through again, but this time with Queen Victoria in attendance, much to her obvious delight. The queen insisted that Robert Lees should become her resident medium at Windsor, but during one of their sittings, Prince Albert communicated with her (through Robert Lees) that his preferred medium was John Brown. John Brown, a gillie on the royal Balmoral Estate and the now famous, in our own time, as well as then, personal assistant to the queen.

So, John Brown became not only a personal attendant, confidant and eventually close friend of Queen Victoria's, but also her royal medium and he acted as conduit between her and her dearly beloved, but sadly departed Prince Albert.

The queen was a prolific writer. From the age of thirteen to 10 days before she died at the age of 81, Victoria wrote in her diary religiously and daily. She noted events in great detail, both personal and professional. Her feelings, thoughts, experiences, secret desires and private dreams. Fascinating content for anyone interested in the inner workings of the queen's mind. The queen who ruled over the British Empire and hundreds of millions of peoples living in it.

What the queen really thought, what she got up to in her private life, her opinions on political events and people in power would indeed be interesting reading beyond comprehension!

She'd been baring her soul privately on paper for over 60 years.

At her death, she'd amassed a total of 122 volumes of her personal journals. It's estimated that she wrote around 2000 words a day — 60 million words in total… 750 novels worth!

Sadly for us, after Queen Victoria died in 1901, all of her hand written journals, at Queen Victoria's request (and without doubt her advisors) and before anyone else could read them, were whisked away by Princess Beatrice, the Queens daughter and literary executor.

Beatrice's job, as literary executor was to re-write the diaries and purge them of any information that might cause embarrassment to the monarchy, current and passed politicians and even the general reputation of the empire itself.

So, the princess re-wrote the diaries, censoring what we might think of today as the most interesting sections as she went!

Beatrice edited the journals down from 122 to 111 volumes.

She removed 11 volumes worth of information. Dozens of novels worth!

Once the mammoth task of editing and re-writing was complete, the majority of the original diaries written over 60 years by the queen were destroyed.

So, we know for certain, judging by the volume of information Beatrice removed that she was utterly ruthless with her editing. But we also have an idea of the kind of topics and sensitive chapters she, and of course her private advisors disapproved of.

One good example of her overzealous editing was where she deleted a diary entry from 1840. This was an entry that had previously been published and so it was known to exist.

It was a record, hand written by the Queen, where she describes taking great delight in Prince Albert putting on her stockings (assumed him putting them on her!) and then Victoria continues to note how she afterwards enjoying watching Albert shave. A highly surprising and intimate insight into a monarch's private life and certainly not the image most people have of Queen Victoria.

Beatrice obviously felt this entry to be far too revealing and personal and so she deleted it from the abridged diaries and attempted to rub it out of the history books. Once Beatrice's job was complete, hundreds of thousands, if not millions of words were removed from Victoria's diaries.

What else she removed, no one knows, or will ever know.

We'll never understand the truth behind the queen's true relationship with John Brown. Was she indeed secretly married to him as many believe? and what about the seances where she and John Brown communicated with Prince Albert. What kind of messages and advice from the other-side did she receive? And what was the true extend of the queen's involvement with spiritualism? These questions and so many more would no doubt have been answered in her unabridged journals.

You can read Beatrice's edited version of Queen Victoria's journals online and they make fascinating reading. They do give an insight into the queen's life as a monarch, but what the diaries obviously lack are what the contemporary reader would see as the best and the juiciest bits of content! The real and even the naughty side of the character and personality of the queen who reigned over the biggest empire the world has ever seen. Those best bits have all been lost in the mists of time and in the flames of a bonfire… she was much more interesting than you think!

Ironically, Queen Victoria, after her death reportedly sent messages from beyond the grave herself. These were to her daughter Princess Louise during organised medium sessions. What was said during these seances has also been very much kept secret!

So, the queen's interest in the super natural was well known and publicised in gossip pamphlets and newspapers. Curiosity then spread throughout society and some highly notable personalities of the time became followers of spiritualism.

Arthur Conan Doyle, better known as the author of the hugely popular, then as now 'Sherlock Holmes' novels was the best known and most out-spoken practitioner of Spiritualism. He openly discussed his beliefs and was often quoted as saying that he was certain that the dead were able to communicate with the living through earthy conduits or mediums.

Conan Doyle was an early supporter of the Spiritualist Association of Great Britain. An organisation still in existence today. The SAGB began life in the 1870's located in and around Marylebone, London. The group was originally called the Marylebone Spiritualist Association.

An interesting location for a spiritualist organisation to begin. Marylebone is an area I mentioned earlier in this book.

As we know, at the time, there was a large community of Anglo-Indian families living there, who'd returned to England from the sub-continent. Like most ex-pats, they felt much happier living amongst like-minded people with similar life experiences, in culture, food and lifestyle. Whether these Anglo-Indian families had any involved or influence over the ideas and development of spiritualism in Marylebone at this time is unknown, but it would seem likely with their long experiences of India and it's ancient historical and cultural connections to spiritualism.

Arthur Conan Doyle was there right at the beginning. Described as the 'Saint Paul of Spiritualism' he dedicated his final years and resources to the cause and in fact expressed a wish that he should be remembered for his psychic work rather than for his novels. This, as we know isn't the case — the author is much better known for his brilliant detective character 'Sherlock Holmes'

However, there is some evidence in the ever-popular novels that Sherlock Holmes used a little spiritualism himself in his crime fighting detection methods. Conan Doyle believed that science and spiritualism went hand in hand. His fictitious character seems to believe that too. In the novels, Holmes is able to pick up an object, weigh it in his hand, move it around, observe it from all angles and from this, deduce the last owner's sex, age, occupation, habits and personality… in exactly the same way as a practitioner of spiritualism!

So, spiritualism was absolutely part of Victorian life, some would say a sub-culture, but there were plenty of available publications dedicated to the subject. Specialist newspapers, magazines, pamphlets, as well as many societies up and down the country (not just in Marylebone) and indeed around the empire.

Spiritualism was available to everyone through these publications and there was no end of supply of professional practitioners who could be invited to hold private seances, sittings and readings.

As you can imagine, there was a great conflict between it and tradition church teachings, but many people genuinely believed and took comfort from it.

However, the reputation and popularity of spiritualism dropped dramatically in the early part of the 20th century. Well known sceptics like Harry Houdini, the famous escape artist, who ironically many believed must have been a spiritualist to be able to perform his amazing feats, investigated and de-bunked claims by the ever-increasing group of practising so called 'spiritualists'. These performers he called them were putting on shows, both privately and publicly in sell-out theatres. Houdini was highly vocal in his disdain for what he described as charlatans who were defrauding grieving customers out of their money.

The subject certainly divided opinions, as it does today. In fact, so much so that Houdini's great friendship with Arthur Conan Doyle came to an end over disagreements about spiritualism!

Another irony is that on the anniversary of Harry Houdini's death (Halloween 1926) and for ten years afterwards, Houdini's wife held seances in an attempt to contact the spirit of her husband. He didn't come through and she eventually gave up, but others haven't. Even to this day, Houdini devotees hold seance rituals each Halloween in an attempt to make contact with the great escape artist. There is still so much interest in this, that visitors are banned from visiting Harry Houdini's grave at Halloween!

One of the most famous Victorian mediums, whom Houdini disapproved of was Florence Cook (1856–1904) She materialised during her seances as a spirit called Katie King. Florence described Katie, as the young spirit daughter a 17th century pirate and the spirit of Katie had a reputation for terrible flirting during seances. She would gently touch and kiss sitters as she wondered around the room… this made Katie quite popular!

Florence Cook herself was pretty popular too and she was invited to many highly respectable Victorian houses for paid private parties. At one such event, whilst in a trance, she was reportedly seen to levitate above the heads of the amazed sitters… just before her clothes fell off!

Free Education

Prior to 1870 in Britain, education was only available to those who could afford it, so children generally received no basic formal education, unless they were lucky to receive charity or church schooling.

The majority of working-class children (like the famous missionary Dr David Livingston, whom, I'll get to soon) went out to work as soon as possible.

But in 1870, the government introduced The Education Act which was the first system of free schooling for children aged between 5 and 10. Costs for the education were paid for by the public through their property rates.

Education at this point was not compulsory and take up for the free education wasn't as enthusiastic as you might think. Many parents simply couldn't afford to allow their children time off work and in turn give up the much-needed income earned by their children.

So, it wasn't until sometime later in 1880 that the government made schooling compulsory for all children... this didn't solve the problem of children being sent out to work though. Truancy rates were very high, due to parents keeping their children off school... so, they could go to work!

The school leaving age over the following years slowly increased from ten in 1870 to fourteen in 1900.

Popular (or not so popular) jobs for children in 19th century Britain

Coal mines: Coal, described as 'black gold' powered the industrial revolution's steam engines and these modern machines brought about great changes in the world and huge benefits to hundreds of millions of people around the world.

However, the miners who dug the coal out of the ground to drive Britain's new industrial revolution didn't feel much of a sense of pride for the work they were doing. And they certainly didn't get much public praise for it either... no matter how beneficial it might have been for others!

Conditions down the pit then were horrendous. Gas explosions, shaft collapses, fires and life-threatening lack of oxygen were daily concerns. Throughout the 19th century over 1000 miners a year died in pit accidents across Britain. Many more died of a multitude of respiratory diseases.

Bad enough for adults, but children were not excluded from the mines. In fact, due to their small size, young boys were needed down the pits and in large numbers. The 'Pit Lads' were able to crawl through tight spaces, pushing and pulling (wearing a 'girdle and chain' similar to a Donkey) the coal wagons along very low tunnels, impossible for grown men to work in and possibly the worst and certainly the loneliest job of all, the young lads were employed as the 'Trappers'. A trapper's job was to sit alone, deep underground for 12 hours at a stint, in complete darkness, often dripping wet, opening and closing trap doors.

These were boys as young as eight whose job it was to wait by the side of a rail track, listening in the pitch black for the sound of approaching coal trucks. Once the truck was close enough, they'd open a trap door, allowing the truck (often pushed by other boys) to pass by and at the same time opening up the ventilation in the tunnel, in an attempt to regulate the air and circulate it around the mine.

Factories

The new factories of the industrial revolution were 24 hour a day operations and Britain was the workshop of the world. It was boom time for the factory and mill owners.

This was the beginning of the modern the 24 / 7 working practise. The 24 hours in the day were spilt into three segments of eight hours. Eight hours work, eight hours recreation and eight hours rest. That was the general principle and it was one designed to get the best out of workers, all of course on rotating shift systems, keeping the factories churning out the goods constantly.

In reality though workers at the bottom of the pile could easily put in shifts of twelve hours or more a day. Children too.

The new, super powered, massive and incredibly noisy machinery that was producing all sorts of fabrics, products and materials required by nations around the globe, needed constant attention to keep them running smoothly and efficiently. Again, children due to their size (boys and girls) were ideal for this working environment. They could squeeze in between machines to maintain engines, fix jammed looms, or run from place to place, ducking under working machinery, carrying supplies on a 'just in time' manufacturing system. The hours were hard, very long and often children slept where they worked in-between shifts.

Accidents and deaths were common, but this was before the Health & Safety Act of 1974!

Of course, children were ideal as chimney sweeps and we know all about that, but the biggest downside for being a child during this time, was being so small (sometime they were under fed to keep them this way). Any job you can imagine that would require a person to be small and agile, no matter how dangerous it was, you'd find a child employed to do it. Including, working in the newly built and high-tech sewer systems of Britain. Blockages were inevitable and who do you think would be best suited for clearing these in particularly tight spaces?

It wasn't unusual for boys as young as 10 to go to sea either. Merchant ships recruited young lads, as did the Royal Navy. In times of war especially, the navy needed 'Powder Monkeys' who'd in battle be able to run quickly back and forth between firing cannons and the gunpowder stores. The supply of powder was kept well away from firing ports for obvious safely reasons. But it was vital in a military engagement for the powder to be at hand the very moment the gunner needed it. The Powder Monkey's job was to keep him supplied, again on a 'just in time' system. A highly important job and one best suited to a very small person who could duck under low beams, jump over obstacles and dive out of the way of flying junks of oak, as the sides of the ship exploded from enemy fire!

It wasn't all that bad at sea though, there were certainly prospects for talented people and the navy was good at spotting them.

Lord Nelson, hero of the Battle of Trafalgar, who saved England from being invaded and conquered by Napoleon went to sea at the age of 12... and thank goodness he did. Napoleon really didn't like the English!

Captain James Cook didn't join the Royal Navy until he was 26. Before that he'd spent ten years on a merchant ship and prior to going to sea, he'd worked on a Yorkshire farm from the age of 13.

James Cook entered navy service as a common seaman, but through obvious ability and skill, he worked his way through the ranks, eventually taking command of his own vessel... and going on to discover Australia!

The luckiest working children were those who found themselves toiling away in the countryside on small farms, working in a family business, or even as a servant for a wealthy household. The super fortunate were the small percentage who gained apprenticeships in one trade or another.

Other jobs including being employed as street vendors, selling everything from newspapers, cigarettes to ribbons. Running errands, carrying messages and even as 'Crossing Sweepers' whose job it was to sweep the road clear of horse dung before a wealthy pedestrian crossed the street!

It all sounds horrific and it was compared to today... we really don't know how lucky we are, or what our ancestors truly had to go through, but it wasn't all doom and gloom for the ordinary folk of the empire.

There are endless examples of people from humble

backgrounds, who with genuine ability and skill broke through and made their mark.

It wasn't the feudal system of old where talent was suppressed in favour of less able people with higher social status. If you had the ability, the drive and the work ethic, there were chances for you to make it in the empire. It was never going to be easy, it certainly wasn't handed to you on a plate, but the British system did value ingenuity, tenacity and talent.

One of the best examples of this is George Stephenson. The man known around the world as 'The Father Of The Railways'

George Stephenson was a coal miner from Newcastle. He came from an impoverished family, had no schooling whatsoever, and so, as a young boy, he did the only thing he could do. He followed his father to work down the local pit. George Stephenson couldn't read or write until he was 18.

Not the best start in life then. However, he shot to international fame in the early part of the 19th century, because George was a genius engineering pioneer, an inventor and a trailblazer. His natural gifts were spotted early on by the coal mine owners. They were nurtured, utilised and profited from. Not through some act of kindness or a sense of moral duty to help those less fortunate either. Far from it, it didn't work that way… it was all about the money!

If you're planning on building an empire, either a world dominating one or just your own small business, you need to employ the very best talent there is. It's quite simple, the empire builders knew this and it didn't matter where the talent came from.

It didn't take long for George to go his own way, set up his own firm making steam powered engines and locomotives.

It's these amazing engines he's particularly celebrated for. The most famous being the wonderfully named 'Rocket'. With an equally brilliant name, there was the lesser-known locomotion called 'Black Diamond' but the loco that takes its rightful place in the history books was 'Locomotion Number 1'

This machine, designed and constructed by George Stephenson revolutionised the way people would travel in the future and forever.

In 1825, Locomotion Number 1 was the first train in the world to pull a passenger car (full of local dignitaries) And just for good measure, attached to the stream engine, there were carts of coal and flour (80 tons worth)

Locomotion Number 1 travelled at 24 miles an hour and for two hours solid (driven by George) along the first railway of its kind in the world, the 'Stockton & Darlington' line in the north east of England.

The pulling power, speed and obvious potential of the machine, at the time, was akin to space age technology to us.

The 27th September 1825 was the official birth date of passenger rail travel and it didn't take long for Britain's towns and cities to be interconnected by the new railways. Fast and safe movement of goods, people, ideas and information fuelled the massive expansion of the industrial revolution and of course the British Empire around the globe... and all thanks to George Stephenson, the 'pit lad' from Newcastle

The Slave Trade

History is complicated, it's layered with contradictions, apposing, sometimes nonsensical and confusing facts. It's a web of stories that can be interpreted very easily to suit any agenda. The subject of the slave trade is one that has more shocking twists and turns, confusions and hypocrisies than almost any other. I'll try to summarise Britain's involvement during the period of the empire.

The slave trade is not a recent historical event (i.e something that only happened a few hundred years ago) It's a trade that is flourishing today in the 21st century and all over the world. Under cover or just under the noses of 'civilised' western societies and in open human slave markets in not so civilised societies. And it's one that has gone unchecked without a single break since the dawn of time.

From the Egyptians to the Romans, The Vikings to the Barbary pirates. The Barbary Pirates were the slave traders from North Africa who from the 16th to the 19th century raided the coasts and waters around Ireland and England (as well as the whole of the Mediterranean) taking Christian slaves to be sold in the markets of Algeria, Morocco, Libya and Tunisia. It's estimated that around one-million Europeans were taken into slavery during this time. Ironically, this was going on during the same period as the biggest human trade ever known. The Atlantic African Slave Trade.

But it's this The Atlantic African Slave Trade in which the British were heavily involved, along with the Portuguese, French, Spanish and Dutch. After the Portuguese, Britain transported more African slaves than anyone else. It's estimated that around twelve million Africans were transported across the Atlantic over a four-hundred-year period and at its height between 1700 to 1807 British merchant ships were responsible for around three million themselves.

The slaves were purchased by British, American and other European traders in West Africa, direct from African dealers and states.

The African merchants ran large wholesale operations, selling captured people to the Europeans. The individuals they sold were taken from opposing tribes and different ethnic groups (wars were waged purely to seize slaves) as well as political opponents from their own tribes.

Once transported, the slaves were again sold in the Caribbean and in the Americas.

Britain without doubt was one of the biggest merchants in the Atlantic slave trade. However, the British public, of whom only 5% at most had any say or vote in such matters, began calling for the end of the trade from around 1780. In Britain the Society for the Abolition of the Slave Trade was set up in 1787. Many smaller organisations had tried previously and failed to make their voices heard, but this group put in place a structure and organisation that mobilised thousands of Britons to speak with one voice against the trade.

Eventually, through 20 years of campaigning, public meetings, petitioning, printing of anti-slavery books, pamphlets and even the manufacture of anti-slave trade promotional artefacts made by companies like Wedgwood pottery (Josiah Wedgwood, the founder of Wedgwood was one of many well-known and prominent abolitionists) the Society for the Abolition of the Slave Trade won the argument and in 1807 The Abolition of the Slave Trade Act was finally introduced... Britain became the first major power in the world to ban slavery.

Further Acts followed and Britain began to use its power to suppress the slave trade throughout the world. The British Government set up naval squadrons to patrol the west coast of Africa and the Caribbean to combat the slave traders. The Royal Navy's West Africa Squadron was the most famous of all and it was specifically set up to fight and stop illegal slave ships in the act of trading. For 60 years the West Africa Squadron did this, but it came at a substantial cost. More than 1500 British sailors died fighting the slave traders and many more were struck down with tropical diseases.

Over the several decades and throughout the 19th century, countless people were saved from ever being traded, 1,600 slave ships were captured and 150,000 slaves freed.

This has been described as 'the most costly international moral action, in modern history'

The British empire wielded its military, commercial and diplomatic power and effectively appointed themselves the anti-slavery policeman of the world. This was not popular with other states like Spain, Portugal and the Netherlands (or the African dealers) who all attempted to continue with the trade. But, through economic pressures, international treaties and threat of military intervention, Britain was able to gradually suppress the slave trade throughout the 19th century. Hard cash also played a role. In 1833 Britain spent 40% of its national budget to buy the freedom of all people still in slavery around the empire. A debt that wasn't fully paid off until 2015... all the above paid for by the British tax payer, both then and now.

Missionaries played a large role in combating slavery too. Compared to most colonialists, they were driven for very different reasons when they went out into the world. Their main aim was to convert the people they encountered to Christianity, but also to spread western civilisation and at the same time bringing commerce in its wake. The intention was to make more people of the world 'British' if they could, or at least a little more British than when they found them! But, with slavery being very common and the norm amongst the nations they came into contact with, the missionaries' dual role and one as important as any other, in fact necessary to achieve the main goals of civilisation, was to abolish slavery where they found it.

Dr Livingstone I presume!

David Livingstone is probably the best known of these imperial missionaries of the 19th century. A driven man, full of conviction, there is no doubt. Brave, certainly, he lived a life of service to others. And, as is often the case from the days of empire, he came from humble beginnings. Born in Blantyre, Southern Scotland in 1813. He began work at the age of ten in the local cotton mill. Working a daily shift of fourteen hours, the monotonous work in the mill, he later admitted taught him 'persistence, endurance and a natural empathy with all who labour' (These were skills he employed exploring Africa some years later)

A life such as this for youngsters, as we know, was not unusual at the time. The free school state education system had not yet been introduced, so it was perfectly normal to send small children out to work in order for them to make a financial contribution to the household and it's running costs.

A tough beginning, but Livingstone's father was a Sunday School teacher and so with many books around the house, the young David Livingstone had access to information and education. He became an avid and accomplished reader.

Luckily too for the young David, was the fact that the mill where he worked had its own basic night-school which was available to workers, but only after finishing their shifts. The school was open between 8pm and 10pm, but most workers didn't have the energy to attend!

So, with several years of hard study at the mill school, reading at home, help and encouragement from his family, David Livingstone was able to enrol at medical college in Glasgow (while still working at the mill to support himself)

Whilst studying medicine, Livingstone also went through theological school and later missionary training.

In 1840, at the age of 27, Dr David Livingstone set off for Africa. He was excited by the new missionary work he'd heard about which was expanding to unexplored lands north of South Africa and by the prospect of bringing an end the African slave trade which was very prevalent there.

Slaves were being traded and sent east from trading ports along the African coast to India, the Middle East, Madagascar and the Americas.

A business that had been thriving for several hundreds of years.

This anti-slavery work would be achieved by Livingstone and others though Christian conversion and hand in hand with that, they'd attempt to substitute the tradition business of 'slave trading' with what they referred to as civilised 'legitimate trade'. This came in the form of western goods, methods and practises. Livingstone also mapped the areas he explored, marking navigable rivers, which were described as and later used as highways into the African interior... all funded by private donations and government grants.

For decades, stories of Livingstone's adventures, achievements and disasters filled newspaper columns — he was once mauled by a Lion, which left one arm crushed and his body scared with eleven permanent big cat tooth marks... much to the delight of the newspaper owners and their readers!

David Livingstone had great regard for the people of Africa. He learnt several African languages fluently and credited his African companions as being indispensable to his work. Without them, he said he could never have completed his journeys. Their zeal and efforts were as great as his in spreading Christianity, commerce, and civilisation — this trinity he believed was the key to abolishing slavery. This was the topic that obsessed him.

As you probably know, Dr David Livingstone went missing for several years. No reported sightings, no dispatches, absolutely nothing… he seemed to simply vanish. All sorts of rumours were spreading. Conspiracy theories as you'd imagine were being regularly written about in the press, but these soon became stale. They were just not the same as real documented exploits from the man himself. This was very bad news for newspaper sales and so there was only one thing for it. Livingstone and his tales of exploration needed to be found.

So, Henry Morton Stanley from the New York Herald was dispatched into the wilderness to find him!

In true investigative journalistic style, Stanley found Livingstone in November 1871 in present day Tanzania with the famous greeting

'Dr Livingstone, I presume?'

Stanley later wrote that he was shocked by Livingstone's appearance. Missionary work had obviously taken a toll on his health. He was drawn, looked far older than his years, and he'd quite obviously been suffering from all sorts of ailments throughout his journeys. From horrific tropical fevers to dreadful haemorrhoids — these were so bad, that they caused Livingstone serious blood loss. Stanley tried to convince him to return with him to Europe or America, even just for a short while to recuperate his health, and especially to have treatment for the haemorrhoids, which were potentially life threatening. Livingstone refused, fortunately though Stanley arrived in Africa bearing gifts of medicines, ointments and supplies. All of which helped David Livingstone a little with his obvious discomfort!

Stanley and Livingstone travelled together for quite some time. Stanley of course asking the questions and scribbling constant notes. You can imagine the sense of excitement Stanley must have felt. He knew that every word he wrote down in the wilderness of Africa would be picked over and devoured by the multi millions of eager readers around the world and as soon as he returned to America.

Livingstone recounted his amazing stories of travel, adventure, discovery and dangers. But especially he spoke about the East Africa Slave Trade and his determination to bring it to an end.

One particular account was shockingly gruesome. This was when Livingstone described to Stanley his time in the Congo where he witnessed a massacre of Africans by Arab slave traders. All of these first-hand stories eventually made it back to the newspaper printing presses in Europe and America. As hoped and expected, they caused outrage and equal amounts of ghoulish intrigue… just as they would today.

Newspapers, bulging with these stories, including Illustrations of the events were selling like hot cakes. But, along with increased newspaper revenues came the realisation that the slave trade was indeed still flourishing. Public awareness turned into real public pressure for something to be done about it.

The British Government then were compelled to take a harder stance and so they were encouraged and expected to 'Send in the gun boats' and cut off one of the main markets supplying slaves to Arabia.

Find and cut off the supply of anything and you effectively stop the trade in whatever product it is. The same principle applied to the East Africa Slave Trade. People from all over Africa were being kept captive, traded and sold in one main market, which was located just off the coast of what is today Tanzania

This place was Zanzibar. The small trading island was the hot spot for the slave trade. Dealers, middlemen, officials and brokers were all making fortunes out of their human commodities. In fact, it was the islands main source of income.

Here, slaves were shipped across from the African mainland to be sold in huge open markets. It was a hub for the business and traders from all over the world would barter for and purchase their human cargo before transporting them, mainly to the Middle East.

Britain had been putting pressure on the Sultan's of Zanzibar to end the trade since the 1820s and a number of anti-slavery treaties had been agreed upon and signed by Zanzibar, but generally, after a period of 'lip service' these were simply ignored.

The Sultan's and the traders side stepped and broke the agreements constantly. However, with the surge in publicity after the Stanley / Livingstone meeting and subsequent interviews, Britain stepped up the pressure with extra Royal Navy patrols along the east coast of Africa.

It was a huge area to cover and slave trading ships were still getting through, including French, Spanish, Portuguese and even American owned vessels. But in 1873, the Sultan was informed that due to the obvious continuation of the trade (and pressure at home) a total blockade of Zanzibar by the British was imminent.

A complete Royal Navy blockade of all trade in and out of Zanzibar would decimate the economy of the island within weeks.

With this in mind, the Sultan agreed to sign a new and permanent agreement. This was the 'Anglo-Zanzibari Treaty' which abolished the slave trade in the Sultan's territories, closed down all slave markets and gave protection to freed slaves.

There are some that argue these days that it wasn't the British who really closed the Zanzibar slave trade down. They say it ended for purely economic reasons. A collapse in the market for certain commodities or crops, that slaves were forcibly used to produce in the Middle East or India. Meaning, a much-reduced need for slaves. It can be said that if the demand for slaves was declining anyway, then this would certainly have influenced the Sultans decision to sign the treaty. But it wouldn't have made economic sense for him to ban the trade altogether, unless the threat from the British was taken seriously.

Either way it was indeed the British that got the final agreement signed, sealed and delivered and this was the agreement which finally closed the slave markets down in Zanzibar.

And, one thing is for certain. Dr David Livingstone (with a little help from Stanley and his newspaper) can take the lion's share of the credit... tooth marks and all!

Less than two years after the meeting with Stanley, at the

age of 60 David Livingstone was dead. He died in Africa of Malaria and Dysentery. His African companions buried his heart in present day Zambia and then carried his mummified body for nine months and over 1000 miles to Dar es Salaam, where it then sailed for Britain.

Dr David Livingstone is buried in Westminster Abbey, London.

Out of interest, it is estimated that today in our modern world, there are 40 million people enslaved... not much changes really.

How about some good old British moral superiority/confidence and self-belief!

If you could bottle and sell in the 21st century what the British created for themselves in the 19th century (confidence, moral superior and self-belief) you'd become a multi-millionaire overnight!

You can do anything, become anything and achieve anything. Nothing is impossible, if you believe you are right, and your acts and deeds are carried out for the right reasons.

The colonialists and adventurers all had 'right' on their side. Imagine you're living in the 19th century for a moment and you'll probably understand how this could be the case. British imperialists, pioneers, explorers, missionaries, government officials and swash bucklers all felt a moral and cultural superiority over other nations.

You might find this unpalatable today, but remember to remind yourself that you're imagining you're living in the 19th century... it was different back then!

Being part of the British empire and the British system,

they believed empowered them (some felt an obligation) to spread across the world the best of British values, of Christianity, civilisation, industrialisation and a system of law, order and responsibility... the conversion of nations, peoples and other cultures to become 'British' was the right way forward, it was believed, for future world peace. A world free of wars, conflict and one full of prosperity and hope.

There were good reasons for thinking this way. Don't forget that the British, especially throughout the 19th century were on a roll, living through a continued purple patch of success... They started the industrial revolution, which, when it comes to revolutions was a very good one indeed. They invented trains, incredible machinery, increased life expectancy, made scientific breakthroughs, developed new medicines, built wealth, bridges, roads, warships and became not just the workshop of the world, but they were at the centre of cutting-edge technological discoveries. London was the Silicon Valley of its day!

On top of this, with their military might, they were also the ruler of the seas and indeed the police force of the world (Note: the British also invented the modern police force)

Whatever they put their minds too, they generally did it jolly well indeed and better than anyone else. In fact, the British at the time were about the best at everything, much to the resentment, envy and immense frustration of competing European powers!

From the Queen at the top of the pile to the workers in the newly industrialised factories, the vast majority of people bought into the British system. It may not have been a completely perfect, or fair system of course, but most people were pragmatic. It was the best available. They knew that the alternatives to the British Empire and its modus operandi were far worse. Despots near and far, around the world would have loved to have stepped in and taken over the reins of the empire if they could. Everyone knew that those snapping at the British Empire's heels didn't have much sense of fair play to put it mildly... not like the one, the British were proud of!

So with this sense of absolute purpose, self-belief and great confidence, off went into the world thousands of Britons to make the world, as they saw it, a better and safer place... and they came from all levels in society too.

Some people (in fact many) did this for purely selfish reasons of course. Opportunists, confidence tricksters and the snake oil salesmen, but many were true believers in fair play and a fair opportunity for everyone who came under the umbrella of the British Empire.

This, by the way was a very long-term plan and it was expected (as 'core shocking' as it may seem to you now) that some groups of people around the globe would take several generations to assimilate, but the dream was that they'd all eventually become good examples of 'Britons' and the world would be a safer place, one great nation, under one empire. I suppose you could call it a model of a British Utopia? ...oh, the pomposity of it all, I'm sure you're thinking.

In fact, the utter arrogance is appalling for the modern reader. Yes, for sure... but this was a very different time to today!

Enter Cecil John Rhodes!

Cecil Rhodes was born in Bishop Stortford, England. His father was a vicar and Cecil was educated at the local grammar school.

He was a sickly child and at the age of 17, suffering from suspected consumption, he was packed off to South Africa to live with his brother who owned a farm there. The warmer climate and outdoors life, it was hoped would be good for his health. Cecil was never really expected to live very long and he suffered his first slight heart attack at the age of 19.

Farming didn't suit Cecil and his brothers farm failed anyway, so Rhodes, with no real experience in business, apart from running the farm, found himself with his brother in the diamond rush and mines of Kimberley. Fortunately for him, he was very good at not only running a mine, but also buying up other mine concessions, diamond dealing, business in general and building a huge company, which soon became the world famous De Beers Diamonds.

While still running his business, Rhodes split his time between South Africa and Oriel College, Oxford where he studied Greek and Latin. He was thought of as being a little odd by his contemporaries there and described as being somewhat eccentric and prone to rambling monologues.

But it was here at Oxford that Rhodes first shared his dream of creating a 'secret society' of British men who would work to become leaders of the world. Their role would be to spread to all corners of the globe British values and the spirit of the Englishman with the sole intention of bringing the whole of the uncivilised world under British rule… including America!

To expand the Empire, was not only for the good of the empire, but, as he believed, it would be beneficial for all peoples over whom it would rule... it was in fact a god given task!

By the time Rhodes was 28 and had graduated from Oxford he was exceptionally wealthy and a member of the Cape Parliament in South Africa. At 34, he was one of the richest men in the world and at 37 he became prime minister of the Cape.

An ardent imperialist, he believed in the rapid expansion in Africa of British interests before competing countries like Spain, Portugal and Germany got there first. He had the money and the determination to do it too. His focus was to paint the map of Africa, British red and connect the whole continent from the Cape to Cairo with a fast and modern railway line, running through all British territories and without ever leaving British territory. Spreading trade, civilisation and building cities as it went. Just like the railways had done in America.

And talking of America, Rhodes really was of the opinion that it would be a very good idea to reclaim the old American colonies, which were lost to Britain in the previous century. This was one of his secret society plans of action!

He was focussed on his African project first though and he was in fact consumed with the idea at almost any cost.

Rhodes was quoted as saying "The object of which I intend to devote my life is the defence and extension of the British Empire. I think that object a worthy one because the British Empire stands for the protection of all the inhabitants of a country in life, liberty, property, fair play and happiness and it is the greatest platform the world has ever seen for these purposes and for human enjoyment"

Most people simply got on with their lives during this time, making a living, getting by as best they could, but some and Rhodes is the best example took the idea of expanding the empire around the world to extreme lengths!

Painting Africa British red, which was his first challenge was going to be a very expensive venture indeed, but Rhodes was as wealthy equivalently then as any of the top social media magnates, or tech billionaires are today. He had immense power in the same way they do too. He was also positively bulging with self-belief. The tenacity, the reputation, credibility, backing and yes, a feeling of moral superiority to boot!

He certainly didn't spend much money on himself. He wore very ordinary clothes and definitely didn't live an ostentatious lifestyle, in fact he lived quite frugally, unless he was entertaining eminent visitors from notable politicians to celebrities. Then, he'd lavish them with parties and luxuries, all of which to cultivate favour, so it was money well spent. And talking of money, he had, or could get his hands on just about all the money in the world for his project.

What he didn't have was time. His health, although earlier improved by the African climate was still poor, so he knew that time was not on his side… this left no time for very much other than his work… what he saw in fact as his 'calling'.

He never married, he had no known female relationships in the traditional sense and it's often suggested that Rhodes was likely homosexual. As we know this was illegal at the time and an imprisonable offence, so if this was the case, it was necessary to keep his sexuality very well hidden… Rhodes certainly would have died in prison.

Cecil Rhodes is, as we know, a highly contentious figure today.

The fact is though, he has never been anything else. Even during his lifetime, at the height of the British Empire, his form of staunch imperialism and theories on cultural evolution (to make everyone British eventually) were attacked and openly criticised, by opposing politicians and newspapers. None of his critics had any power to stop him though and in reality, they didn't half love talking about him!

As did the public, who loved to read about him in the press. He was a larger-than-life character, a real shocker, but a compelling one.

A hot topic around the empire and elsewhere and he seemed happy enough to be loathed, envied and admired in equal measures!

Rhodes really was a 'love or hate him' character in his lifetime and no different in that regard to famous politicians and the super powerful today. He divided opinions around the empire and would often appear as a caricature of himself in publications all over the world and not just in colonial countries either. The French hated him, he was a thorn in the side of their imperial ambitions and so they loved to mock him and his big ideas! The Germans and Portuguese didn't take kindly to Rhodes either. He blocked their African ambitions too. All this publicity though worked out quite well for Rhodes. The more the world talked about him, and even ridiculed him, the more he rubbed people up the wrong way, the more they gave him publicity and fame, the more traction and credence is ideas gained!

He was quoted as saying that "The British race was the finest in the world and the more of the world they inhabited, the better it would be for the human race". That was his belief and he believed that through his actions, he was bringing benefits to Africa. That can be argued today of course and it is on a huge scale, but at the time, he had faith (believed God given) in these convictions. He was focussed on his plan and he certainly didn't hide it — what he hoped to bring to pass was no secret... and millions of people around the world agreed with the general ideals of it... And just as many, hated him for it!

To achieve his dream of improving the world with British influence and cultural evolution, he was as utterly ruthless in his actions as he was thought to be brilliant. A famous tycoon, a focussed imperialist and a feared politician.

He bought his way, traded, signed treaties and fought mini wars (he was even partially responsible for the second Boer War) to achieve that dream. Nothing it seemed was going to stop him... apart from his health.

Rhodes died of heart failure in 1902 at the relatively young age of 48. In reality he lived longer than anyone had expected due to his health conditions, but he never did realise that dream and ambition of turning the whole of Africa from the Cape to Cairo British, or bringing those renegade Americans back into the fold of the empire!

His last few years were blighted with illness, which he didn't help by refusing to rest. Legal battles, disappointments and scandals held him up too. It was a race to finish what he'd started and it was a race he lost. However, he did get a country named after him (Rhodesia) and he added 450,000 square miles to the Empire.

He died in Cape Town, but he'd decided some years earlier to be buried in Rhodesia, the land that was named after him (now Zimbabwe) in the Matopos Hills, Matabeleland. A sacred, royal place for the Matabele and for the Karanga people whom the Matabele had conquered seventy years earlier, after they too had trekked north from South Africa and over the Limpopo River. But now, the new conqueror of the land would join the other chieftains buried in those venerated hills. The same place in fact where Rhodes held talks with Lobengula, the Matabele King... whom he later went to war with and defeated!

Rhodes said in life that he wanted to cheat the constraints of mortality by leaving a legacy. The legacy he was ideally thinking about was the one in which he'd leave Africa, the whole of the continent and its people 'British', expend British influence around the world and reclaim the USA, but this was not the legacy he left!

Apart from the obvious legacy of his controversial life, Rhodes left a sum of money in his will, which created what we know as the 'Rhodes Scholarship' This was a cash fund which amounted to around 12.5 million pounds today.

The scholarship was open initially only to young men (this being before women were encouraged into further education and before the Suffragettes made their mark) The scheme enabled these male students from all parts of the British Empire, plus America and Germany to apply. If successful, the scholarship paid for them to study at Oxford University. The aim being to promote unity within the empire and leadership marked by public spirit and good character and to "render war impossible" by promoting friendship between the great powers.

The scholarships and the criteria are based on Rhode's final will and testament. It states that "No student shall be qualified or disqualified for election on account of his race or religious opinions"

The Rhodes Scholarship was and still is one of the most prestige academic awards in the world. Recipients include

American President Bill Clinton, Pakistan's president Wasim Sajjad, Prime Ministers of Australia Tony Abbot, Bob Hawke and Malcolm Turnbull. Prime Minister of Jamaica Norman Manley and of Malta Dom Mintoff. Then there are the scientists, Nobel prize winners, musicians, journalists, entrepreneurs and philanthropists.

Cecil John Rhodes will continue to be a much-discussed character from history and his words and deeds have been and will continue to be dissected and scrutinised. Ironically, this was all part of his plan and intended legacy. To continue to engage in open discussion, in argument and debate would, he said, improve the world. And the criteria he demanded from the recipients of the 'Rhodes Scholarships' included not just the highest academic standards, but for leadership skills, a keen interest in others and a devotion to duty. All of which was to deepen the scholars understanding of other people... as he said "to broaden by their acquaintance with one another and by the exposure to cultures different to their own" which would he hoped bring stability and peace to the world... but, all under British control of course!

We're now coming to the end of the book, and coincidentally, we're living through the end of the British Empire. The Commonwealth will likely last indefinitely and you might find this an odd thing to say, but empires, especially the biggest one ever known to man take a very long time to burn out... and we're all, even now, living through the burn out stage!

Like fashions, empires don't just exist one day and not exist the next. For example, in recent history, it took Bell-bottom trousers several months to slowly become unfashionable. As it happens, most people didn't realise this for a few years, but you get my point.

And as a point of interest: in the early part of the 19th century American sailors in the US Navy started wearing rather fetching Bell-bottom trousers. The British Navy in good traditional empire style, nicked the idea for their own sailors in the mid-19th century, but we won't dwell on that. Empires make mistakes!

Empires then are no different to fashion, they have a life span, a beginning, a middle and an end, but with empires they take generations to dwindle away, not months and in fact their influence and legacy can last forever.

The British, have left their mark all over the world. The most obvious being physically in the form of structures, from 19th century shopping arcades in Hong Kong to Parliament buildings in India. Railways, roads and bridges of course, but it wasn't just infrastructure they left as evidence of their existence. They left behind systems of government, judiciary, education, sports, a spirit of 'Britishness', the English language and yes even a jolly good postal system!

In fact, the postal system is a good analogy to make here when it comes to talking about the demise of the empire. In 1900, at its height, we know, the British Empire's postal system had as many as 12 deliveries a day, with the first arriving at 7.30 in the morning. It was cheaper, more efficient and more reliable than it is today too! We still use the same old red post boxes, as do many ex-colonial countries around the world, but the postal service both in Britain and elsewhere is a shadow of what it once was... just like the empire!

And sticking to that particular time line as an example and comparison. In 1900 school children were taught that they, as members of the British Empire, if they employed whatever talent they had, they could achieve anything, do anything and be anything they dreamed. They'd be expected to work hard, to be brave, adventurous and embrace a sense of fair play and daring. But being born British, they believed that they were very lucky indeed. This gave them an advantage in life over all other nations and cultures. They were taught to be proud and patriotic, no matter what social class they came from. Teachers generally now take an opposite view!

Some of you may well be feeling highly uncomfortable here, thinking that this all sounds just too jingoistic for today's delicate ears. Well, yes, it does in the modern world, but it didn't then and this was all part of what made the empire so successful. The empire was very good at building confidence, self-belief, a strong work ethic and courage. A sense of British superiority, to be blunt!

And before you start complaining about these historical facts on social media: just for a moment, compare the British Empire's modus operandi to what the best and most expensive motivational speakers around the world practise and teach us today. Either in seminars, online courses, or in books. These motivational gurus tell us that happiness and success is all about learning to develop and train yourself to be a greater person. To coach your brain in the art of positive thinking, personal empowerment, leadership, confidence and self-belief... an all-encompassing 'can do' attitude to life, which improves not just your life, but crucially, others around you... that's what they promise. By you being 'great' and 'loving yourself' you will enhance the lives of others too!

We are told we need to develop and in fact master these virtues if we want to succeed in love, work, play and life in general... and judging by the eye watering amounts of money these speakers charge and the millions of books they sell, I'm guessing that modern people today quite like the idea of being motivationally trained!

But as ever, not much is really very new in life... and when it comes to motivational training, confidence building and instilling self-belief, The British Empire did it better than anyone else has ever done before or since... And they proved that their training system didn't half work too!

You can't get the old 'Empire Training' these days, but if you want to cultivate a bit of the 'feel good, can do anything' spirit to enhance your life, you might consider going to a motivational seminar or buying one of the many books available... it's probably money well spent!

But back to the decline of the old empire. Yes, we're all going through it and we're close to the end of the final chapter. The Empire is no longer spread-eagled across the world, it's shrunk back to the mother country and it's now in the final stages of fizzling out. This is where its people become increasingly divided (The same happened to the Romans). They lose their collective and individual confidence as citizens of their country and while they squabble about the past, develop self-inflicted guilt complexes and shout at history, they compliantly wait for the next incarnation of an empire to come along... which it will... it's just the way it happens.

The British Empire then, no longer controls the territories it once did. The sun that was so proudly described as never setting over her, now sets every day and as early as 4pm in the winter months!

But, finally, the legacy lives on, because as much as some of you will be horrified and others deeply proud to hear this... We are all products, in one way or another, of the British Empire!